Collector's Encyclopedia of

Flow Blue

CHINA

Second Series

Mary Frank Gaston

COLLECTOR BOOKS
A Division of Schroeder Publishing Co., Inc.

The current values in this book should be used only as a guide. They are not intended to set prices, which vary from one section of the country to another. Auction prices as well as dealer prices vary greatly and are affected by condition as well as demand. Neither the Author nor the Publisher assumes responsibility for any losses that might be incurred as a result of consulting this guide.

On the cover:

Left, Vase, American, $400.00 – $500.00. Top right, Soup Tureen, Vermont, $400.00 – $500.00. Middle right, Pitcher, Salisbury, $100.00 – $120.00. Bottom right, Pitcher, Josiah Wedgwood, $400.00 – $500.00.

Searching For A Publisher?

We are always looking for knowledgeable people considered experts within their fields. If you feel that there is a real need for a book on your collectible subject and have a large comprehensive collection, contact Collector Books.

Cover Design by Beth Summers
Book Design by Joyce Cherry

Additional copies of this book may be ordered from:

Collector Books
P.O. Box 3009
Paducah, KY 42002-3009
or
Mary Frank Gaston
P. O. Box 342
Bryan, Texas 77806

@$24.95. Add $2.00 for postage and handling.

Copyright: Mary Frank Gaston, 1994.
Prices updated 1996

Printed by IMAGE GRAPHICS, INC., Paducah, Kentucky

To Jerry and Jeremy

Other Books by Mary Frank Gaston

The Collector's Encyclopedia of R. S. Prussia
The Collector's Encyclopedia of R. S. Prussia, Second Series
The Collector's Encyclopedia of R. S. Prussia, Third Series
The Collector's Encyclopedia of Limoges Porcelain, Revised Second Edition
Blue Willow, Revised Second Edition
The Collector's Guide to Art Deco
Antique Brass and Copper

Contents

Acknowledgments

A large number of individuals have made this *Second Series* of *The Collector's Encyclopedia of Flow Blue China* possible. Patterns and pieces not shown in my 1983 edition were requested when I contacted collectors for help with this new book. The response was very rewarding, and I am pleased to be able to show such a range of patterns and objects which would not have been possible if I had personally photographed all of the examples. I extend my most sincere thanks to the contributors listed below who photographed patterns and marks and provided other pertinent information for each piece. I also thank those who have sent documentation for unidentified patterns or manufacturers shown in the earlier book. I hope this *Second Series* will serve to further the interest of these and other advanced collectors and will also attract new enthusiasts to the pleasures associated with collecting Flow Blue China.

Thanks are extended once more to the contributors to the first edition. Some examples from those contributors have been reprinted to correct pattern names or manufactures. Several pieces, from some of those contributors, which were not included in that book are shown here.

Contributors to the *Second Series*

Bill and Sandy Alley, The Apple Tree Mall, Branson, Missouri
Susan Anastasio
F. R. Anderson
Carleen Andre´- Rogers, Chico, California
Jeanette Bader
Marla Betz, Forest City, Iowa
Clara R. Casper, Warren, Michigan
June Chance, Sacramento, California
Nancy Cottrell
Betty DeKeyser
Betty French, Leslie, Michigan
JuDeane Garrett, Mableton, Georgia
Richard C. and Sondra Green, Pottstown, Pennsylvania
Peggy Grotts, Bixby, Oklahoma
Merle and Grace Harris, Golden Eagle Bazaar, Yountville, California
Freda Hines, Salem, Missouri
Margaret Hoeft, Grand Island, Nebraska
Rajayne Hoffmann
Claire M. Hopkins
Horseshoe Antiques, Saguache, Colorado
Tim and Janis Hunt, Garland, Texas
Malorie Hunt, Pensacola, Florida
Betty Hurley, Hebron, Indiana
Lorraine Kohlbeck
Becky Korbel
Pam and Ralph Krainik, Seven Gables, Baraboo, Wisconsin
Shirley Krantzberg
Joseph and Fern Krisman, Caspian, Michigan
Ruth Lehman
Kim McKinney, Sierraville, California
Virginia Metcalf, South San Francisco, California
Mrs. E. R. Meyersick, Pendleton, Oregon
M. Clydene Miles and Martha Card, Seabrook, Texas
Earlene Moore, Hamilton, Alabama

Richard Muscott, Ionia, Michigan
Helen Nelson, Turon, Kansas
Elta Olson
James S. Pitcher
Lawrence R. Reno
Jean Riecker, Northville, Michigan
Shirley Seitz, Millville, New Jersey
Cindie Smith
Sue and C. Aubrey Smith, Jr.
Danell Smith-Wright, Pleasanton, California
Theva C. Stevens, Hyndsville, New York
Dave Taylor, Decorah, Iowa
Doris L. Thompson
David Turner, Munster, Indiana
Patricia Brophy Wall and Patterson Wall, South Pasadena, Florida
Charles and Dorothy Washer, Bloomingdale, Illinois
Virginia Avis Whitham, Ionia, Michigan
Brad and Eunice Witt
Diana and Ted Wood, Milton, England
Juanita Zinn, Great Falls, Virginia

Contributors to the *First Series*

Dorothy and Elmer Caskey, Covington, Ohio
Joyce Brown, Prairie Wind Antiques, Frederick, Oklahoma
Crawford's Antiques, San Antonio, Texas
Mr. And Mrs. Phil Cummins, Joshua, Texas
David Dodgen, Houston, Texas
Gladys M. Donham, Houston, Texas
Dunn & Ross Antiques, Houston, Texas
Arvena Fleury, O-P Book Shop and My House Antiques, #136, Trade Mart, Houston, Texas
Georgia Harris, Weathervane Antiques and Show Promotions, Columbus, Texas
Don and Charlene Johnson, Golden Age Antiques, Pawnee, Oklahoma
Professor and Mrs. William L. Hendricks, San Francisco, California
Suzanne King, Nottingham, England
Irene and Marc Luther
Vera McLeod, Curiosity Antique Shop, Big Spring, Texas
Lois Misiewicz, Fallbrook, California
Carolyn and Max Allen Nickerson, Nickerson's Antiques, Eldon, Missouri
Shirley Porter, The Antique Key, #40 & #41, Trade Mart, Houston, Texas
Connie Rogers, Dayton, Ohio
Lloyd Ward Antique Shows, Euless, Texas
Floris and Carl Walton, Grandfather's Trunk, Deland, Florida
Marceline White, The Chinaberry Tree, Stowell, Texas

Introduction

Ten years have passed since my first book on Flow Blue China was published. While there is no doubt that this type of ceramic ware was extremely popular in 1983, interest in Flow Blue has not only continued but steadily increased during the interim. Evidence of this is apparent from the amount of Flow Blue found for sale at antique shops and shows across the country. Auction houses specifically indicate "Flow Blue" in their listings to entice buyers. A number of businesses throughout the United States specialize in Flow Blue and serve as matching services for the china. In 1986, an International Collectors Club was organized. The club publishes a bi-monthly newsletter and holds an annual convention.

Flow Blue continues to be a very active blue chip investment. Unusual pieces and rare patterns fetch extremely high prices, but the basic table ware items, which composed the bulk of this type of china production, also command sums on par with, or sometimes more than, fine porcelains. Although many collectors concentrate on assembling a set of patterns and pieces made during the mid 1800s, later patterns and pieces made during the 1900s are gaining in popularity. This is in part a response to the scarcity and price of the older pieces. Later made examples, however, also merit collecting.

Due to the popularity of Flow Blue, an assortment of reproductions are also being produced. Such items were available ten years ago, but the amount has increased. Many of these are made in England and imported here through wholesale houses. Lack of knowledge regarding pottery marks and history of the china often causes new collectors to purchase these pieces. Price, however, may be one of the best clues that an item is not authentic. Reproductions are usually priced at a much lower figure than genuine Flow Blue. Like other types of current reproductions, buyers should be wary of low prices and an abundance of the same type of objects offered for sale by one shop or dealer. For example, when an antique outlet or flea market has several Flow Blue cheese dishes for sale which have the same pattern and the same mark and are priced for about $30.00 each, it should be obvious that the dishes are reproductions.

Collectors from around the United States and two from England submitted photographs for this *Second Series*. Patterns and pieces not shown in the first book were selected for this edition. Examples of some patterns shown in the earlier book were included in order to show a different piece with a particular pattern. Flow Blue patterns often have a different look depending on the type of object. Some pieces may not have the full pattern. Several patterns which were unidentified either by pattern name or by manufacturer have been reprinted because examples have been found with either the pattern name or a specific manufacturer's mark.

The *Second Series* is arranged in a format similar to the first book. Manufacturers' marks precede the photographs of patterns and pieces. Marks from the first edition have been reprinted with the addition of a number of other marks which were on newly found examples. The old marks were reprinted because many of the new examples were marked with one of those marks. In this edition, the marks are in color, rather than in black and white.

In the first edition, English marks preceded marks of factories from other countries. The English marks were arranged in alphabetical order by factory. The marks of factories from other countries were arranged in alphabetical order by name of country and within country by name of factory. All marks, English and non-English, were numbered consecutively.

The consecutive numbering presented a bit of a problem for this Series. The new marks needed to be placed between the old marks or, two sets of marks would be needed. The latter method could prove to be confusing. Thus, the marks remain numbered in consecutive order, but the new marks have been sandwiched between the old marks. The new marks have either a lower or an upper case letter (abc, ABC) in addition to the number. If the mark is simply an additional mark for a factory, the lower case letter was used. If the mark is for a different factory, an upper case letter was used. For example, mark 11a is merely an additional mark for the Henry Alcock Company. Mark 11A, however, is a new mark for this edition representing the John Alcock factory. Mark 11A is placed between Mark 11a (Henry Alcock) and Mark 12 (John and George Alcock).

Some unidentified marks in the first edition now have been identified. Therefore those marks have been placed under the proper factory name. The old number for the mark has been assigned to a new mark. For example, Mark 79 in FB1 has seen changed to Mark 14a, an additional mark for Samuel Alcock. ("FB1" is used as an abbreviation in this *Second Series* to refer to information in the first edition.) Mark 79 now shows a mark for the James Kent Company.

The captions of the photographs refer to a particular mark number which can be found in the Marks section which precedes the photographs of patterns and pieces. Dating information for a mark is noted in the caption of the mark.

Dating information for English marks is primarily based on Geoffrey Godden's *Encyclopedia of British Pottery and Porcelain Marks* (1964) or on J. P. Cushion's *Handbook of Pottery and Porcelain Marks* (1980). Unmarked examples are noted as being unmarked, and some marks are described if a photo of trademark was not available. A few examples have the notation of being similar to a particular mark. Please note that, as in the first edition, only the marks found on a piece of Flow Blue shown in either the first book or this edition are illustrated in the Marks section. That section does not include all of the marks used by a particular factory, even though several marks may be shown here for one factory.

Patterns made by English manufacturers are presented in alphabetical order by pattern name in the first section of photographs. Some of these patterns are referenced to one of Petra Williams's books on Flow Blue. When an unmarked pattern appeared to match an identified pattern in one of those volumes, the pattern name was used. This same method was used in my first edition, but those pattern names were printed in lower case letters within quotation marks. All English patterns in the *Second Series*, however, are printed in capital letters.

A number of English patterns are not marked with a particular name. In my earlier book, if an example did not have a documented pattern name or an obvious popular name the pattern was listed as unidentified. In this edition, I have included a few names for patterns which Ms. Williams assigned to such unmarked examples. Over the years, these patterns have not surfaced with a factory name, and collectors use the assigned names. A larger number of patterns are identified by popular names in this book. Flow Blue patterns which are unmarked as to pattern name, but the design clearly suggests a name, have been listed under that popular name. Quite a few patterns, however, are still listed under the unidentified category. I have not attempted to assign names to those patterns. Perhaps by showing these, documented names may be brought to my attention.

The second set of photographs contains examples of unidentified patterns made by English factories. The third group of pictures includes completely unmarked samples. There is no pattern name or factory mark on these pieces. The majority appear to be of English origin, however.

Handpainted Flow Blue, popularly referred to as "Brush Stroke," is featured in the fourth section of photographs. Most of these patterns are of English origin, and most of them are unmarked as to pattern name or manufacturer. Some popular names, often more than one, are associated with some of the patterns. Most of these popular names have evolved from names used by Petra Williams to identify such patterns in her books. While those popular names were not used in FB1, some are used in this edition. Collectors do find names useful for identification and communication purposes.

Some of the handpainted patterns also have the addition of copper lustre to the pattern, and others are polychromed designs. "Gaudy" is often the term used for such polychromed pieces and also represents a separate category of collectible ceramics. A few examples in this section appear to be non-English in origin, and that is noted in the caption for the item. Some pieces are also decorated with a combination of handpainted and transfer work.

The fifth section of photographs focuses on Flow Blue made in non-English countries. The examples are arranged by name of country in alphabetical order. American pieces are shown first. In FB1, such examples were placed under the heading of the United States. The sixth and final set of pictures includes some modern reproductions of Flow Blue china. A few of the marks found on these pieces are also shown.

A list of Flow Blue patterns shown in this *Second Series* has been included. The patterns are listed in alphabetical order with a photograph number to serve as a handy index. The list is for both English and non-English patterns and contains some popular names for some patterns. The list of Manufacturers' initials and Ambiguous Marks has been expanded in this edition. A list of Objects is also indexed by photograph number.

The *Collector's Encyclopedia of Flow Blue China, Second Series* is designed to catalog, in color photographs, additional patterns and pieces from those shown in the first edition published in 1983. Collectors are referred to that book for discussions of the history of the china, types of marks, and definitions of terms associated with Flow Blue. This second book does not complete the cataloging of all Flow Blue patterns. Collectors are invited to send photographs of patterns which are not found in either of my books.

Mary Frank Gaston
P.O. Box 342
Bryan, TX 77806

Please include an SASE if a response is required.

Flow Blue Pattern Names
(Numbers refer to color plates)

English Manufacturers and their Patterns

Non-English Manufacturers and their Patterns
(Numbers refer to color plates)

American
Crescent Pottery 421
The French China Co. ....423 – 430
Imperial China Co. (Pioneer Pottery) 431
Knowles, Taylor, Knowles 432
Mercer Pottery 433, 434
Oliver China Co. 435, 436
Sebring Pottery Co. 437
Sterling China Co. 438, 439
Warwick China Co. ....440 – 442
Wheeling Pottery Co. 443
Unidentified 422, 444, 447

French
Keller & Guerin ....448 – 450

Utzschneider & Co. 451
Unidentified 452

German
Reinhold Schlegelmilch 453
Royal Bonn 455, 456
Unidentified 454, 457, 461

Holland
Unidentified 462

Sweden
Gefle ....463 – 465

Non-English Patterns

Eglantine 448
La Belle 443
Luzerne...434
Paisley..433
Pansy 440
Parapette 450
Persian Moss...457
Pilgrims Landing 430, 431

Spinach 430, 431
Turkey 435, 436
Utopia 421
Vinranka ....463 – 465
Wild Rose ....455 – 456
Winona ....422 – 424
Others ....425 – 428, 431, 432, 437 – 439, 441, 442,
    444 – 447, 449, 451 – 453, 458 – 462

Manufacturer's Initials

B. B. ....Minton (Best Body)
B. & C. ....Burgess & Campbell (American)
B. & K. ....Barker & Kent
B. & L. ....Burgess & Leigh
B. & S. ....Bishop & Stonier
B. W. M. & Co. ....Brown-Westhead, Moore & Co.
C. & H. ....unidentified
C.T.M. ....C. T. Maling
D. ....Thomas Dimmock
E. B. & J. E. L. ....Bourne & Leigh
E. C. ....Edward Challinor
E. P. C. ....Empire Porcelain Co.
F. A. M. (monogram) ....F. A. Mehlem, Germany
F. & Sons ....Ford & Sons
F. & W. ....unidentified
F. W. & Co. ....F. Winkle & Co.
G. B. (monogram in star shape) ......Grimwade Bros.
G. & S. ....Grove & Stark
H. ....Hackwood
J. & E. ....Mayer (American)
J. E. ....John Edwards
J. F. & Co. ....Jacob Furnival & Co.

J. H. ....Joseph Heath
J. H. W. & Sons.........................J. H. Weatherby
J. P. Over L. ....Jean Pouyat (Limoges, France)
J. R. B. ....John Ridgway, Bates & Co.
J. & T. F. Co. ....Jacob and Thomas Furnival
K. & Co. ....Keeling & Co.
K. & G. ....Keller & Guerin (French)
K. T. & K. ......Knowles, Taylor, Knowles (American)
L. & A. ....Lockhart and Arthur
M. & B. ....Minton and Boyle
M. & Co. ....Mintons
M. & H. ....Minton & Hollins
M. V. & Co. ....Mellor, Venables & Co.
N. W. P. ....New Wharf Pottery
P. (monogram in circle)..........................unidentified
P. H. ....Peter Holdcroft
P. W. & Co. ....Podmore, Walker & Co.
R. & M. (under Coat of Arms) .....Ridgway & Morley
R. & M. Co. ....Rowland & Marsellus (American)
S. A. & Co. ....Samuel Alcock
S. & E. H. ....unidentified
S. F. & Co. ....Samuel Ford

Ambiguous Marks

Objects

(Numbers refer to color plates)

English Marks

1. William Adams & Sons, circa 1819 – 1864.

2. William Adams & Sons, circa 1819 – 1864.

2a. Williams Adams, circa mid 1800s.

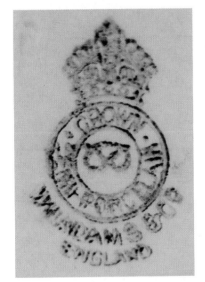

3. William Adams & Co., England, after 1891.

4. William Adams & Co., England, after 1891.

5. William Adams & Co., England, after 1891.

6. William Adams & Co. , England, after 1891.

7. William Adams & Co., England, after 1891.

7a. William Adams & Co., after 1891.

8. William Adams & Co., Tunstall, England, after 1896.

9. William Adams & Co., Tunstall, England, after 1896.

10. William and Thomas Adams, circa 1866 – 1892.

10 a. William and Thomas Adams, circa 1866 – 1892.

11. Henry Alcock & Co., England circa 1891 – 1900.

11a. Henry Alcock & Co., Stoke-on-Trent, England, circa 1910 – 1935, in green with a pattern mark in blue.

11A. John Alcock, Cobridge, circa 1853 – 1861.

12. John and George Alcock, Cobridge, circa 1839 – 1846.

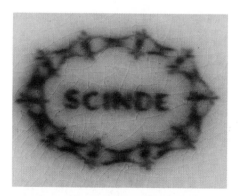

13. John and George Alcock, impresssed initials with "Oriental Stone" circa 1839 – 1846.

14. Samuel Alcock & Co., initials, circa 1830–1859.

14a. Samuel Alcock, initials, circa 1830 – 1859. (Correction for Mark 79 in FB1.)

15. Charles Allerton & Sons, England, after 1891 and probably before 1912.

16. Allertons, mark in banner under crown, England, circa 1903 – 1912.

17. Ashworth, G. L., impressed crown with name, circa 1862 – 1880.

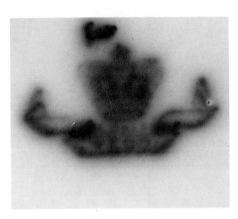

18. Ashworth, G. L. & Bros., crown with A. Bros. and banner underneath, circa 1862 – 1890.

19. Ashworth, G.L. & Bros., lion over scroll with G.L.A. Bros. and pattern name, circa 1862 – 1890.

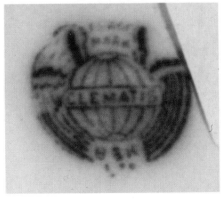

19A. Barker & Kent, initials, circa 1898 – 1941.

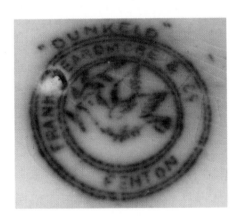

19B. Frank Beardmore & Co., Fenton, circa 1903 – 1914.

20. Bishop & Stonier, "Bisto," circa 1891 – 1936.

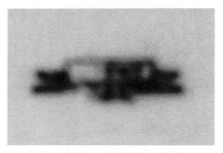

20a. Bishop & Stonier, initials, circa 1891 – 1910.

20A. T. & R. Boote, initials, circa 1842 – 1890.

21. Bourne & Leigh, "E. Bourne and J. E. Leigh, Burslem, England" plus initials, circa 1892 – 1939.

22. Bourne & Leigh, "Albion Pottery," plus initials "E. B." and "J. E. L., " circa 1912 –1941.

22A. Sampson Bridgwood & Son, England, circa 1891 – 1933.

22B. British Ware, unidentified manufacturer.

23. Brown-Westhead, Moore & Co., Cauldon, England, circa 1895 – 1904.

24. Burgess & Leigh, Middleport Pottery with initials, after 1889 to 1919.

25. Burgess & Leigh, Middleport Pottery, England, circa 1891 – 1919.

26. Burgess & Leigh, Burslem, England, circa 1906 – 1912.

27. Burgess & Leigh, Middleport Pottery, Burslem, England, circa 1906-1912.

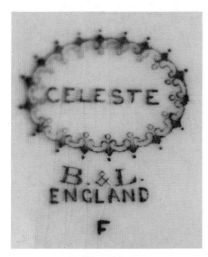

28. Burgess & Leigh, initials with England, circa 1891 – 1919.

28A. C. & H., Tunstall, England, unidentified manufacturer, circa after 1891.

29. Cauldon, England, circa 1905 – 1920.

30. E. Challinor, circa 1842 – 1867.

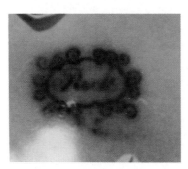

30a. E. Challinor, initials circa 1842 – 1867.

31. Possibly Edward Clark, circa 1877 – 1887.

31A. J. Clementson, circa 1840 – 1864.

32. Clementson & Young, circa 1845 – 1847.

33. Alfred Colley, Ltd., Tunstall, England, circa 1909 – 1914.

33a. Alfred Colley, Ltd., Tunstall, England, circa 1909 – 1914.

33A. C. Collinson & Co., Burslem, circa 1851 – 1873.

33B. W. T. Copland, England, circa after 1891.

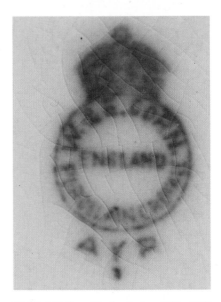

34. W. & E. Corn, "Porcelain Royal, " circa 1900 – 1904.

35. W. & E. Corn, monogram with "Porcelain Royale Art Ware, England," circa 1900 – 1904.

36. W. & E. Corn, England, circa 1900 – 1904.

37. Davenport, impressed anchor mark, circa early 1800's to circa 1860 for this type of mark. The one shown here is for 1844 with an impressed "4" on either side on the anchor.

37a. Davenport, printed mark with impressed anchor mark, year cypher illegible, after 1805.

38. Dean, S. W. & Co., circa 1904 –1910.

39. Dimmock, Thomas, circa 1828 – 1859.

39a. Dimmock, Thomas, initial, Crown mark with pattern name, circa 1828 – 1859. (Correction for Mark 138 in FB1.)

40. Doulton & Co., circa 1882 –1890.

40a. Doulton & Co., Burslem, circa 1882 – 1890.

41. Doulton & Co., England, circa 1891 – 1902.

41a. Doulton & Co., England, circa 1891 – 1902.

42. Doulton & Co., Burslem, England, circa 1891 – 1902.

43. Doulton & Co., Burslem, England, circa 1891 – 1902.

43a. Doulton & Co., England, circa 1891 – 1902, with artist's mark.

44. Doulton & Co., Royal Doulton, England, circa 1902 – 1930.

44a. Doulton & Co., Royal Doulton, England, with U. S. patent date (June 5th, 1906).

45. Doulton & Co., Royal Doulton, Burslem, England, circa 1902 – 1930.

46. Doulton & Co., Made in England, after 1930.

47. Doulton & Co., Royal Doulton, Made in England, after 1930.

47A. Dudson, Wilcox, & Till, Hanley, England, circa 1902 – 1926.

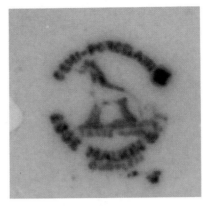

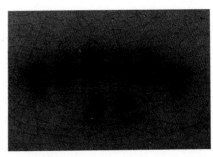

48B. John Edwards, initials, circa 1847 – 1873.

48A. Edge, Malkin, & Co., Burslem, circa 1873 – 1903.

48. E. W., particular company not identified.

49. T. Edwards, particular company not identified, may be Thomas Edwards, circa 1839 –1841.

49A. Empire Porcelain Company, England, circa 1912 – 1928.

49B. F. & W., unidentified manufacturer, marking under pattern name illegible, circa mid to late 1800s.

50. T. Fell & Co., circa 1830 – 1890 , printed initials with impressed "Real Iron Stone."

50A. Samuel Ford & Co., B. Ltd., Lincoln Pottery, England, circa 1898 – 1939. (Correction for Mark 112 in FB1.)

51. Ford & Sons, circa 1893 – 1907.

51a. Ford & Sons, initials, Burslem, circa 1893 – 1907.

52. Ford & Sons, Ltd., circa 1908 – 1930.

52a. Ford & Sons, Ltd., Burslem, England, circa 1908 – 1930.

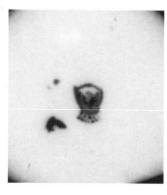

52A. Thomas Forester & Sons, Ltd., Eagle mark with "T. F. & S., England," circa 1891 – 1912.

53. Jacob & Thomas Furnival, circa 1843, printed initials.

53A. Jacob Furnival, & Co., initials, circa 1845 – 1870.

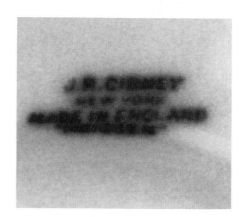

54. Thomal Furnival & Co., circa 1844 – 1846, printed initials.

55. Furnival & Sons, printed in upper part of mark, circa 1871 – 1890.

55a. Thomas Furnival & Sons, impressed name and anchor mark, with "J. R. Gibney, New York," importer mark, circa 1878.

56. Grimwade Bros., initials printed, circa 1886 – 1900.

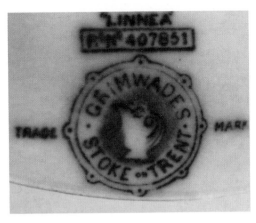

57. Grimwades, after 1903, profile of a lady in center of mark.

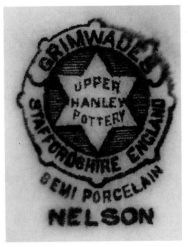

58. Gimwades, circa 1906 and after.

59. W. H. Grindley & Co., England, circa 1891 – 1914.

60. W. H. Grindley & Co., England, circa 1891 – 1914.

61. W. H. Grindley & Co., England, circa 1914 – 1925.

61a. W. H. Grindley & Co., variation of Mark 61, circa 1914 – 1925.

61b. W. H. Grindley & Co., variation of Mark 61a with a U. S. patent date of 1906.

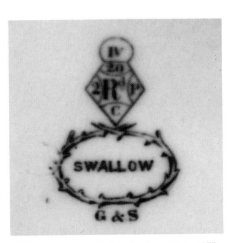

61A. Grove & Stark, initials, circa 1871 – 1875.

62. H. Bros., Tunstall, England, after 1891, no company identified.

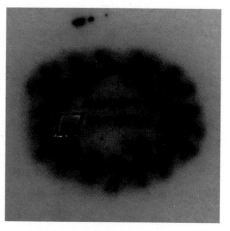

62A. "H" initial, probably Hackwood (see Godden, pp. 289 – 299), circa early to mid 1800s.

63. Sampson Hancock & Sons, Stoke-on-Trent, England, circa 1906 – 1912.

64. Sampson Hancock & Sons, England, initials, circa 1906 – 1912.

65. Sampson Hancock & Sons, England, initials, circa 1906 – 1912.

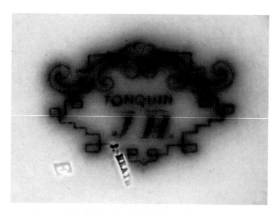

66. J. Heath, printed initials and impressed "J. Heath," probably Joseph Heath, circa 1845 – 1853 although Godden notes that there were other J. Heaths working in Staffordshire at the same time.

66A. Peter Holdcroft & Co., initials, circa 1846 – 1852.

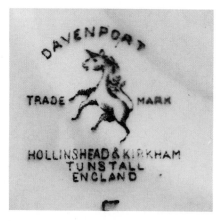

67. Hollinshead & Kirkham, Tunstall, England, circa 1900 – 1924.

68. Thomas Hughes, Longport, England, circa 1860 – 1890.

68a. Thomas Hughes & Son, England, circa after 1895 – 1910.

69. Thomas Hughes & Son, Ltd., England, circa 1910 – 1930.

70. Johnson Bros., England, circa 1900 and after.

71. Johnson Bros., England, circa 1900 and after.

72. Johnson Bros., England, circa 1900 and after.

73. Johnson Bros., England, circa 1913 and after.

74. Samuel Johnson, Ltd., Britannia Pottery, circa 1913 – 1931.

75. G. (or C.) Jones, England, may be George Jones.

76. George Jones & Sons, circa 1864 – 1907.

77. Keeling & Co., circa 1886 – 1891, initials.

78. Keeling & Co. Ltd., circa 1912 – 1936.

79. James Kent, England, circa 1910.

80. Lockhart and Arthur, initials, circa 1855 – 1864.

81. John Maddock, impressed mark with name and castle and "Ironstone China," circa 1842 – 1855.

82. John Maddock, printed oriental style mark with same impressed mark shown in Mark 81. (This mark clearly shows the pattern name and replaces old Mark 82 in FB1.)

83. John Maddock and Sons, England, circa 1880 –1896.

83A. C. T. Maling, initials, circa 1859 – 1890.

83B. C. T. Maling, & Sons, "Cetem Ware, Made in England," circa 1908.

83C. Charles James Mason, circa mid 1800s.

84. T. J. & J. Mayer, Longport, initials, circa 1843 to probably mid 1850s.

85. T. J. & J. Mayer, initials, circa 1843 to mid 1850s.

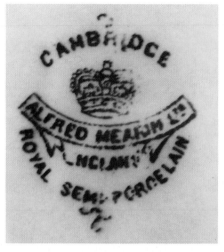

86. Alfred Meakin, Ltd., circa 1897 – 1930.

87. Alfred Meakin, Ltd., circa 1907 – 1930.

88. J. & G. Meakin, Hanley, England, after 1890.

89. J. & G. Meakin, Hanley, England, circa 1890 and after.

90. J. & G. Meakin, Hanley, England (written in mark under crown), circa 1912 and after.

91. J. & G. Meakin, England, circa 1912 and after.

92. Charles Meigh or Charles Meigh & Son, impressed mark "Improved Stone China" in rectangle, circa 1835 – 1861.

93. John Meir, initials which may be "I" or "J M.," circa 1812 – 1836.

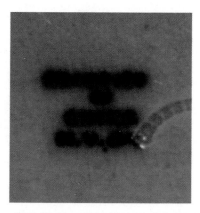

93A. Mellor, Venables, & Co., initials, circa 1834 – 1851.

94. Minton & Boyle, initials, circa 1836 – 1841 impressed "B.B." and "New Stone."

94A. Minton, initials "M. & Co., " circa 1841 – 1873.

94B. Minton & Hollins, "M. & H." initials with impressed mark of "BB, New Stone," circa 1845 – 1865.

95. Mintons, impressed name and registry mark, this type of mark is circa 1873 – 1891.

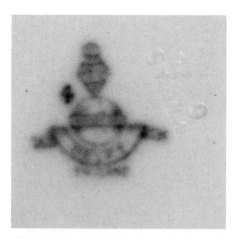

95a. Mintons, printed mark with impressed mark, circa after 1873.

96. Myott, Son & Co., initials under crown, circa 1900 and after.

97. Myott, Son & Co., circa 1907 and after.

97A. Newport Pottery Co., circa 1920s.

98. New Wharf Pottery Co., circa 1890 – 1894.

99. New Wharf Pottery Co., circa 1890 – 1894.

100. New Wharf Pottery Co., circa 1890 – 1894.

100a. New Wharf Pottery, England, Beehive and Urn Mark, circa 1894 – 1900.

100A. "P" monogram mark, unidentified manufacturer (possibly Pilkington Tile & Pottery Co., see Godden, p. 404), circa early 1900s.

101. George Phillips, circa 1834 – 1848 for type of mark.

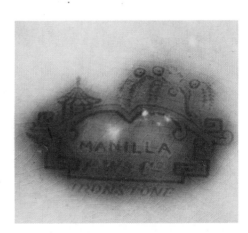

102. Podmore, Walker & Co., initials in oriental style mark, "P. W. & Co." with "Ironstone" underneath, circa 1834 – 1859.

103. Podmore, Walker & Co., "Pearl Stone Ware" written in outer circle of mark with pattern name inside and "Wedgwood" in ribbon underneath, circa 1849 – 1859.

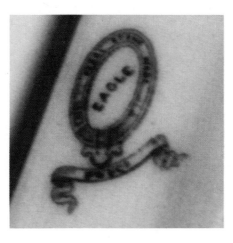

103a. Podmore, Walker & Co., variation of Mark 103, circa 1849 – 1859.

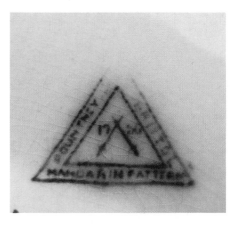

104. Poutney & Co. Ltd., printed name in triangle shaped mark with "Bristol" and name of pattern, crossed swords with "1750" inside triangle, circa 1900 and after.

105. T. Rathbone & Co., initials, circa 1912 – 1923.

105a. T. Rathbone & Co., initials (without "England"), circa 1912 – 1923.

105A. John Ridgway, Bates & Co., initials, circa 1856 – 1858.

106. Ridgway & Morley, coat of arms with initials "R & M" underneath, circa 1842 – 1844.

107. William Ridgway, initials, circa 1830 – 1834.

108. Ridgways, Beehive and Urn mark, England, after 1891 to circa 1920.

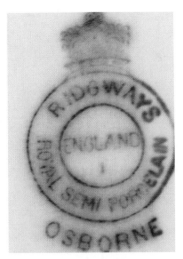

109. Ridgways, circa 1905 – 1920.

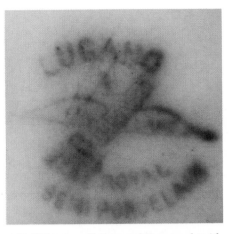

110. Ridgways, Quiver and Bow mark with "Ridgways" on quiver and "England" inside bow and "Royal Semi Porcelain" underneath, circa 1912 – 1920. This mark without England may have "Stoke-on-Trent" which dates from 1880.

111. Rowland & Marsellus, initials, American importing company. This mark does not represent an English manufacturer, circa mid to late 1800s. (Correction for Mark 111 in FB1.)

111a. Rowland & Marsellus, Staffordshire, England, American importing company as in Mark 111 with full name printed. Note the second American importing mark for "Ravis," St. Louis, Missouri.

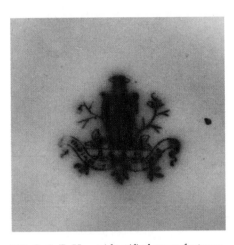

112. S. & E. H., unidentified manufacturer, circa mid 1800s.

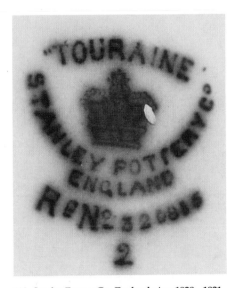

113. Stanley Pottery Co., England, circa 1928 – 1931.

114. Thomas Till & Sons, circa 1891 – 1928.

115. Upper Hanley Pottery, England, printed in mark under crown, circa 1895 – 1900.

116. "W" in diamond shape, England, company not identified, after 1891.

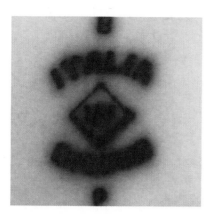

116a. "W" in diamond shape, England, variation of Mark 116. (Note different style of "W.")

117. "W" in diamond shape with England above mark, company not identified, after 1891.

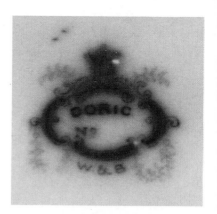

118. W. & B., initials under crown with ornate design featuring pattern name, unidentified manufacturer.

119. E. Walley, impressed mark with name and registry mark in circle, wording in bottom half of mark illegible, circa 1845 – 1856.

120. J. H. Weatherby & Sons, initials, circa 1892 and after.

121. Wedgwood & Co., England, circa 1890 – 1900.

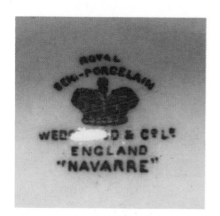

121a. Wedgwood & Co., Ltd., England, circa 1900 – 1908.

122. Wedgwood & Co., Ltd., England, circa 1908 and after.

123. Josiah Wedgwood, impressed name with upper case letters and "PEARL" impressed, circa 1840 – 1868.

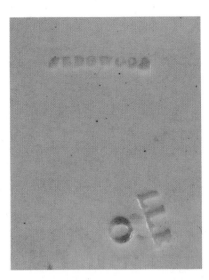

124. Josiah Wedgwood, impressed "WEDGWOOD" in upper case letters with impressed letters of "LLE" indicating date of 1876.

124a. Josiah Wedgwood, Etruria, England, after 1900.

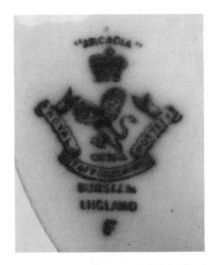

125. Arthur J. Wilkinson, "Royal Staffordshire Pottery" in ribbon beneath lion and crown, Burslem, England, circa 1907.

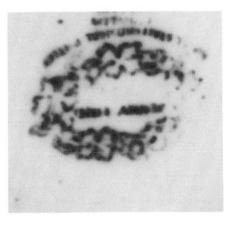

126. Arthur J. Wilkinson, "Royal Staffordshire Pottery, Burslem, England" printed under ornate floral mark containing pattern name, circa early 1900s.

126a. Arthur J. Wilkinson, "Royal Staffordshire Pottery, Burslem, England," circa early 1900s.

127. Wiltshaw & Robinson, initials, circa 1894 – 1957.

128. F. Winkle & Co., initials, circa 1890 – 1910.

128a. F. Winkle & Co., England, circa 1890 – 1910.

128b. F. Winkle & Co., variation of Mark 128.

129. F. Winkle & Co., initials with "Colonial Pottery, Stoke, England," circa 1890-1925.

130. John Wedge Wood, printed "J. Wedwood" on ribbon at bottom of mark, circa 1841-1860.

131. Wood & Son, England, circa 1891-1907.

132. Wood & Son, England, circa 1891-1907.

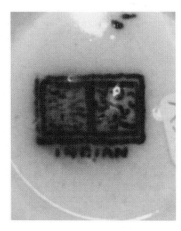

133. Chinese style printed mark with "Indian" pattern name, unidentified manufacturer.

134. Ornate scroll and floral mark, company not identified, "Chinese Pagoda" pattern.

135. Pattern name "Lahore" with England, after 1891, company not identified.

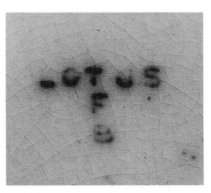

136. Printed "Lotus, F B," company not identified.

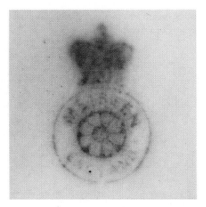

137. Crown and circle mark with pattern name "Meissen" and "England," after 1891, company not identified.

138. "Ocean," pattern mark, unidentified manufacturer, circa mid to late 1800s.

139. Printed mark with pattern name "Sobraon," company not identified.

140. Printed mark with pattern name "Simlay," company not identified.

141. Crown and circle mark with lion and pattern name "Watteau," and "Staffordshire, England," after 1891, company not identified.

142. Impressed crown mark, company not identified.

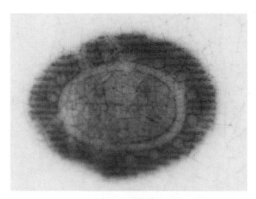

143. Printed mark of oval shape, composed of inner circle and horizontal lines, company not identified.

Non-English Marks

144. Jean Pouyat, Limoges, France, initials, circa 1891 – 1914.

145. Keller and Guerin, Luneville, France, after 1891.

146. Utzchneider & Co., Sarreguemines, France, circa 19th century.

147. "W" in diamond shape with "Quebec" as pattern name and "Germany," company not identified, after 1891.

148. Crown and shield mark, "Made in Germany," possibly Utzchneider & Co., 20th century mark.

149. F. A. Mehlem, Germany, impressed mark, 19th century.

150. F. A. Mehlem, Germany, printed mark, initials, Germany, after 1891.

150A. Royal Bonn, Germany, circa late 1800s to early 1920s.

151. Villeroy & Boch, Germany, initials, mid 19th century.

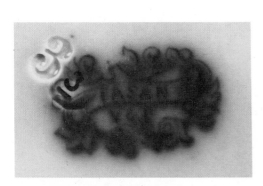

152. Villeroy & Boch, Germany, initials, mid 19th century.

153. Petrus Regout, Maastricht, Holland, 20th century mark.

154. Societie Ceramique, Maastricht, Holland, 20th century mark.

155. T. A., Made in Japan, company not idenitified, 20th century mark.

156. Gilman & Company, Portugal, after 1891, company not identified.

157. Libertas, "Prussia," company not identified.

158. Burgess & Campbell, Trenton, New Jersey, company established in 1879.

159. Burgess & Campbell, Trenton, New Jersey, after 1879.

160. Burgess & Campbell, Trenton, New Jersey, impressed mark with names and lion in circle.

161. The Colonial Pottery, East Liverpool, Ohio, circa 1903 – 1929. (Correction for FB1, see Lehner, 1988, p. 100.)

161A. Crescent Pottery, Trenton, New Jersey, circa early 1900s. (Note Registry Mark in imitation of English marks; also this mark is very similar in style to one used by the George Jones' English factory.)

162. The French China Co., Sebring, Ohio, circa 1900 – 1916.

163. The French China Co., Sebring, Ohio, circa 1900 – 1916.

164. J. & E. Mayer, Beaver Falls, Pennsylvania, company established 1881.

165. Mellor & Co., Trenton, New Jersey, established circa 1894.

166. Mercer Pottery Co., Trenton, New Jersey, established in 1868.

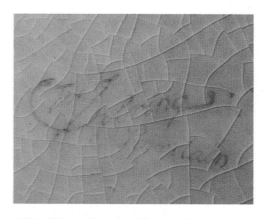

166A. Sebring Pottery, Sebring, Ohio, circa late 1800s to early 1900s.

167. Wheeling Pottery Co., Wheeling, West Virginia, after 1893.

168. Wheeling Pottery Co., Wheeling, West Virginia, after 1893.

English Patterns

PLATE 1. ABBEY, George Jones, Mark 76. Chocolate Pot, 10"h.

PLATE 2. ACORN, Furnivals, Ltd., circa 1910. Soup Plate, 10"d.

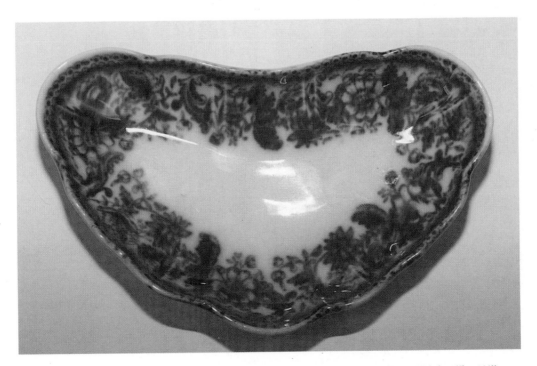

PLATE 3. AGRA (border pattern), F. Winkle and Co., Mark 128a. Bone Dish, 6"l x 3½"w.

PLATE 4. ALASKA, W. H. Grindley, Mark 59. Oval Bowl, 9"l.

PLATE 5. ALBERT, Dudson, Wilcox & Till, Ltd., Mark 47A. Plate 7"d.

PLATE 6. ALBION, W. & E. Corn, Mark 36. Soup Plate, 10"d.

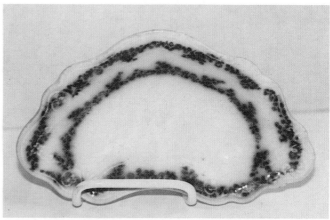

PLATE 7. ALDINE, W. H. Grindley, Mark 59. Bone Dish, 6½"l.

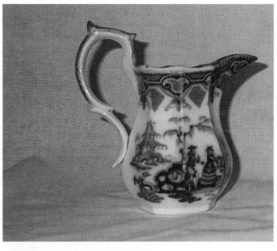

PLATE 8. ALPHABET or ABC Plate, William Adams & Co., Tunstall, England, circa after 1896 (mark not shown). Plate, 6¼"d, center decoration of "Fox and Grapes," apparently a theme based on Aesop's Fables.

PLATE 9. AMOY, unmarked, attributed to Adams, 19th century. Pitcher, 7"h.

PLATE 10. AMOY, additional view of the pattern on the Pitcher in preceding photograph is shown.

PLATE 11. AMOY, Davenport, Mark 37 (pattern identified for Plate 364 in FB1). Covered Sugar Bowl, 8½"h.

PLATE 12. AMOY, Davenport, Mark 37 (pattern identified for Plate 365 in FB1). Tea Pot, 9½"h.

PLATE 13. AMOY, W. E. & Co. (see Godden Mark 1485, William Emberton & Co., circa mid 1800s). Pitcher, 6½"h.

PLATE 14. ANEMONE, Lockhart & Arthur, Mark 80 without the initials "L & A." Pedestal Sauce Bowl with handles.

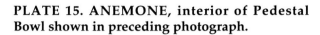

PLATE 15. ANEMONE, interior of Pedestal Bowl shown in preceding photograph.

PLATE 16. ARUNDEL, Doulton, Mark 43. Salad Bowl with silver rim.

PLATE 17. ARUNDEL, Salad Fork and Spoon matching Salad Bowl shown in preceding photograph.

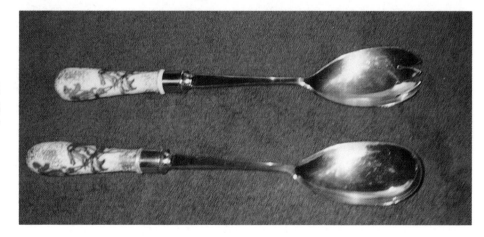

PLATE 18. ASHBURTON, W. H. Grindley, Mark 59. Demi-tasse Cup with pedestal base.

PLATE 19. ASHBURTON, W. H. Grindley, Mark 59. Plate, 9"d.

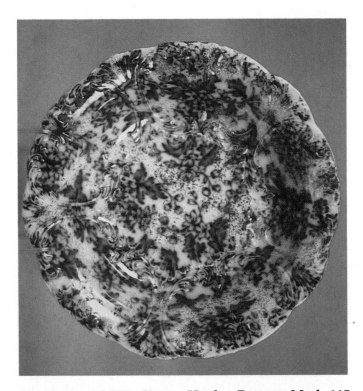

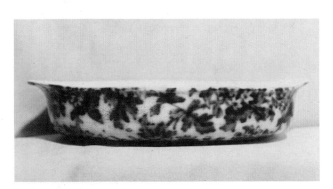

PLATE 21. ASTORIA, Upper Hanley Pottery, Mark 115. Oval Bowl, 11½"l x 6½"w.

PLATE 20. ASTER, Upper Hanley Pottery, Mark 115 (pattern name identified for Plate 372 in FB1). Vegetable Bowl, 10"d.

PLATE 22. ASTORIA, New Wharf Pottery, Mark 98. Pitcher, 6¾"h.

PLATE 23. BAY, Ford & Sons, Ltd., Mark 52. Round Bowl.

PLATE 24. BAY, Ford & Sons, Ltd., Mark 52. Cup.

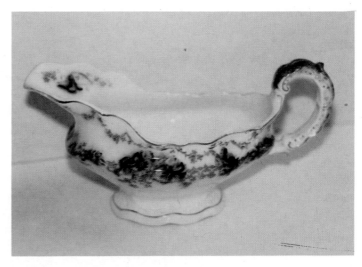

PLATE 25. BEATRICE, John Maddock, Mark 83. Gravy Boat, 9"l.

PLATE 26. BEAUTIES OF CHINA, Mellor, Venables & Co., Mark 93A. Pitcher, 7½"h.

PLATE 27. BEAUTIES OF CHINA, Mellor, Venables & Co., Mark 93A. Plate, 9½"d.

PLATE 28. BEJAPORE, George Phillips, Mark similar to 101. Tureen, 12"h x 15"w; Platter, 18"l x 14"w; Ladle, 12½"l.

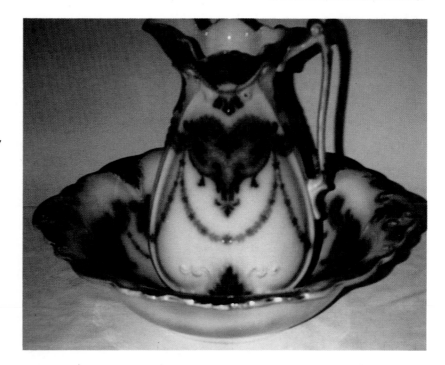

PLATE 29. BELMONT, W. H. Grindley,
Mark 59. Bowl and Pitcher to Wash Set.

PLATE 30. BELMONT, Alfred Meakin, Mark 86.
Covered Waste Jar, 16"h x 14"w.

PLATE 31. BENTICK, John Ridgway (see Godden
Mark 3257, circa 1830 to 1841, crown and coat of arms
mark with "Stone Ware," initials "J.R.," and pattern
name). Platter, 17"l x 14"w.

PLATE 32. BENTICK, Cauldon, Mark 29 (Godden, p. 133, notes that this factory added its name to some of the earlier John Ridgway marks; thus this example of "Bentick" is later than the platter shown in the preceding photograph). Gravy Boat with Underplate, 8½"l x 6 ¼"w.

PLATE 33. BENTICK, marked "CAULDON, ENGLAND," circa 1905-1920 (correction for Plate 368 in FB1). Tureen with polychromed Flow Blue decor.

PLATE 34. BISLEY, W. H. Grindley, Mark 61a. Plate, 9"d.

PLATE 35. THE BLUE DANUBE, Johnson Bros., Mark 73. Saucer, 6½"d, gold trim on border with gold enhancement of design.

PLATE 36. BLUE ROSE (see Williams I, pp. 89 and 106), W. H. Grindley, Mark 60. Fruit or Dessert Bowl, 5"d.

PLATE 37. THE BOLINGBROKE, Ridgways, Mark 110. Plate, 10"d, design embellished with gold.

PLATE 39. BOTANICAL, Minton & Co., Mark 94A. Covered Toothbrush Holder.

PLATE 38. BOMBAY, Thomas Furnival & Sons (see Godden Mark 1649, circa 1818-1890). Demi-tasse Cup.

PLATE 41. BURLEIGH, Burgess & Leigh, Mark 27. Sauce Tureen, 5"h x 8"w with Underplate, 7¾"l x 5¼"w, gold trim.

PLATE 40. BRUNSWICK, New Wharf Pottery, Mark 98. Cup, 3½"h and Saucer, 5¾"d.

PLATE 42. BURMESE, T. Rathbone & Co., Mark 105 (initials and "England" without Swan). Serving Dish, 13½"l x 9"w, pierced handles, ornately scalloped border, gold trim.

PLATE 43. BURSLEM BERRIES, Newport Pottery Co., Ltd., Mark 97A. Gravy Boat with pedestal base.

PLATE 45. CALIFORNIA, unmarked except for Registry Mark of April 2, 1849, attributed to Podmore, Walker, & Co. Tea Pot, 8½"h.

PLATE 44. CALIFORNIA, Podmore, Walker & Co., Mark 103a with "Wedgwood" in banner below mark and Registry Mark for 1849. Plate, 10"d.

PLATE 46. CALIFORNIA, unmarked except for Registry Mark of April 2, 1849, attributed to Podmore, Walker, & Co. Cup with pedestal base, 3"h.

PLATE 47. CAMPION, W. H. Grindley, Mark 59. Bowl and Pitcher to Wash Set.

PLATE 48. CAMPION, Waste Jar matching preceding Wash Set (lid missing).

PLATE 49. CAMPION, Chamber Pot with Cover.

PLATE 50. CANTON, John Maddock, Mark 81. Demi-tasse Cup, 2½"h.

PLATE 51. CARLTON, John and George Alcock, Mark 13. Tea Pot, 8½"h.

PLATE 52. CASHMERE, Ridgway & Morley, Mark 106. Plate, 7"d.

PLATE 53. CATTLE SCENERY, W. Adams & Sons, circa mid 1800s (mark not shown). Round Bowl, 22"d; Oval Bowl, 19"lx 14"w, scalloped border.

PLATE 54. CATTLE SCENERY, unmarked. Cup and Saucer, beaded border. The three examples illustrate three different versions of the pattern.

PLATE 55. CELESTE, unidentified manufacturer, Mark 116. Waste Bowl for Tea Set, 5¾"d x 5½"h.

PLATE 56. CELESTE, John Alcock, Mark 11A. Platter 10"l x 7"w.

PLATE 57. CELESTIAL, John Ridgway & Co., "J. R." initials in oval shape with crown, circa 1841. Pitcher, 7"h.

PLATE 59. CHATSWORTH, K. & Co. for Keeling & Co., circa after 1886 (see Godden Mark 2243). Oval Soap Dish, 9½"l x 6"w; very dark cobalt blue color.

PLATE 58. CHATSWORTH, Ford & Sons, Mark 51. Plate, 10¼"d.

PLATE 60. CHAING or CHANG, unmarked (see Williams II, p. 76). Cup, straight sides, 3"h x 2¾"d.

PLATE 61. CHERUBS, unmarked (English origin). Plate, 9"d, polychromed center decoration of cherubs with a wide cobalt blue border.

PLATE 62. CHINESE SPORTS, unmarked (see Williams III, p. 5; pattern features one figure doing a hand-stand and another dancing with cymbals). Cup, pedestal base and ring shaped handle.

PLATE 63. CHINESE SPORTS, interior view of Cup in preceding photograph.

PLATE 64. CHINTZ, illegible impressed mark. Bowl, 14½"d; Pitcher, 12"h.

PLATE 65. CHISWICK, Ridgways, Mark 109. Saucer with smooth edge.

PLATE 66. CHISWICK, Ridgways, Mark 109. Plate, 10"d, scalloped edge.

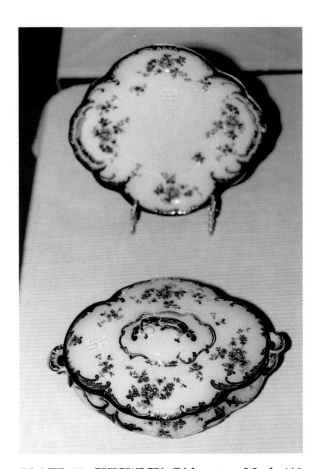

PLATE 67. CHISWICK, Ridgways, Mark 109 with Registry number 295284, circa 1897. Serving Platter, 10"d; Covered Vegetable Bowl, 8½"d, scalloped edges.

PLATE 68. CHUSAN, P. H. & Co., attributed to Peter Holdcroft & Co., Mark 66A. Saucer.

PLATE 69. CHUSAN, C. Collinson & Co., Mark 33A. Pitcher with pedestal base, 11"h; this pattern is the same as the version by Holdcroft in the preceding photograph.

PLATE 70. CHUSAN, J. Clementson, Mark 31A. Covered Sugar Bowl, 8"h.

PLATE 72. CLAREMONT, Johnson Bros., Mark 70. Plate, 10"d, the pattern is the same as ANEMONE by Lockhart & Arthur.

PLATE 71. CIMERIAN, John Maddock, Marks 81 and 82 (pattern identified for Plate 190 in FB1). Soup Plate, 11"d.

PLATE 73. CLAREMONT, Johnson Bros., Mark 70. Covered Vegetable Bowl, floral designs outlined in gold.

PLATE 74. CLAREMONT, interior of Vegetable Bowl in preceding photograph.

PLATE 75. CLAREN-DON, Henry Alcock, Mark 111. Oval Platter, 18"l x 13½"w.

PLATE 76. CLAYTON, Johnson Bros., Mark 70. Soup Bowl, 7½"d.

PLATE 77. CLEMATIS, Barker & Kent, Mark 19A. Vase, 8"h.

PLATE 78. CLEOPATRA, E. Walley, Mark 119. Fruit Compote, 9"h x 13"w.

PLATE 79. CLEOPATRA, unmarked except for pattern name but also attributed to E. Walley. Cake Stand, 2⅝"h x 11¾"d.

PLATE 80. CLIVE, T. Rathbone & Co., Mark 105a. Pitcher, 8"h.

PLATE 81. COBURG, marked with the initials "B & K," attributed to Barker & Kent, see Mark 19A. Platter, 13"l x 10½"w.

PLATE 82. COBURG, Barker & Kent, Mark 19A. Sauce Tureen, 7½"l x 4¾"h; Underplate, 8½"l x 6"w; Ladle, 7"l.

PLATE 83. COBURG, John Edwards, mark 48B. Cup Plate, 4½"d.

PLATE 84. COBURG, John Edwards, impressed initials "JE" with "Warranted." Plate, 8"d.

PLATE 85. COLUMBIA, Clementson & Young, Mark 32. Sugar Bowl, pedestal base, (lid missing).

PLATE 86. COREY HILL, unmarked except for pattern name (pattern identified for Plate 353 in FB1). Pitcher, 11"h, polychromed.

PLATE 87. COREY HILL, unmarked except for "England" on Tray. Dresser Set: Tray, 12½"l x 10"w; Candle Holder; 2 Covered Boxes; Hair Receiver; Pin Tray; and Ring Tree, polychromed.

PLATE 88. COUNTRYSIDE, H. J. Wood (see Godden Mark 4266, Staffordshire Knot with initials, circa 1884). Tea Pot decorated with a windmill and cattle.

PLATE 89. COUNTRYSIDE, reverse side of Tea Pot shown in preceding photograph; pattern composed of rural buildings and a man feeding chickens.

PLATE 90. CRESCENT, W. H. Grindley, Mark 59. Soup Tureen, 7"h x 14"l, pattern is lightly embellished with gold designs. See the following four photographs for other pieces in this pattern.

PLATE 91. CRESCENT, W. H. Grindley, Mark 59. Vegetable Bowl, rectangular shape, 10"l x 8"w.

PLATE 92. CRESCENT, W. H. Grindley, Mark 59. Cake Plate, 14" x 13¼".

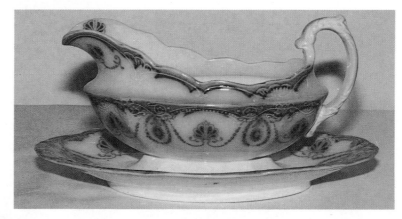

PLATE 93. CRESCENT, W. H. Grindley, Mark 59. Gravy Boat with Underplate, 9"l x 4"h.

PLATE 94. CRESCENT, W. H. Grindley, Mark 59. Soup Plate with gold lustre designs added to pattern.

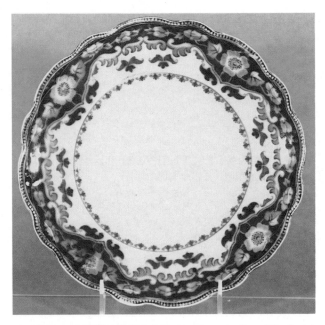

PLATE 95. CRUMLIN, Myott, Son & Co., Mark 96. Soup Plate, 9"d.

PLATE 96. CYPRUS, John Ridgway, Bates, & Co., Mark 105A. Bowl, 10½"d.

PLATE 98. DAHLIA, "E. C." initials with pattern name within a leaf shape, attributed to Edward Challinor, see Mark 30a for initials. Platter, 10¾"l x 8¼"w.

PLATE 97. DAGGER BORDER, unmarked (see Williams II, p. 39, attributed to Thomas Dimmock circa 1844). Cake Plate, 10¼"d; pattern is outlined in gold.

PLATE 99. DAHLIA, unmarked, but also attributed to Edward Challinor. Covered Sugar Bowl, 7½"h.

PLATE 100. DAISY, Burgess & Leigh, similar to Mark 27 with Registry Number 272768, circa 1896. Butter Pat.

PLATE 101. DELAMERE, Henry Alcock, similar to Mark 11. Cereal Bowl, 6½"d.

PLATE 102. DELAMERE, unmarked, attributed to Henry Alcock. Cup, 2½"h, pattern enhanced with gold.

PLATE 103. DELFT, Mintons, Mark 95a. Plate, 9"d. This is the same pattern as DELPH shown in the following two photographs.

PLATE 104. DELPH, illegible factory mark. Plate, 9"d; Cup, 3"h, pedestal base.

PLATE 105. DELPH, unmarked. Cake Stand, 7½"d, pedestal base, gold trim.

PLATE 106. DEVON, unmarked, same pattern as one made by A. Meakin, circa 1907 to 1930, see Plate 86 in FB1. Covered Sugar Bowl, 4"h, 5"d.

PLATE 107. DEVON, Ford &
Sons, Ltd., Mark 52. Covered
Vegetable Dish, 9"l x 6½"w with
Tray or Underplate, 10"l x 8"w.

**PLATE 108. DOREEN, W. H.
Grindley, Mark 60 (pattern identified for Plate 378 in FB1). Chamber Pot with Lid. Other pieces in a
Wash Set are shown in the following three photographs.**

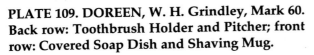

PLATE 109. DOREEN, W. H. Grindley, Mark 60.
Back row: Toothbrush Holder and Pitcher; front
row: Covered Soap Dish and Shaving Mug.

PLATE 110. DOREEN, W. H. Grindley, Mark 60. Wash Bowl and Pitcher Set.

PLATE 111. DOREEN, W. H. Grindley, Mark 60. Covered Waste Jar.

PLATE 112. DORIC, unidentified manufacturer, Mark 118. Platter, 19¾" x 15⅝".

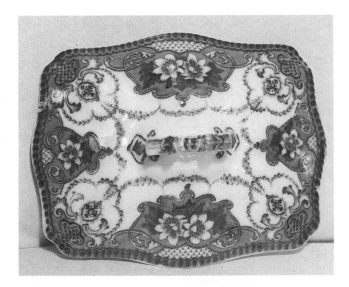

PLATE 113. DOUGLAS, Ford & Sons, similar to Mark 51. Covered Vegetable Dish, 11"l x 8"d (full view of lid to show pattern).

PLATE 114. DOWN THE LONG STREET SHE PASSED, impressed mark of "Wedgewood," which is probably a mark used by William Smith, circa after 1848 until 1855 (see Godden Marks 3598 and 3600). The piece also has the additional printed mark "Made for the Linton & Sinclair Co." Plate, 8½"d.

PLATE 115. DRESDON, Johnson Bros., Mark 70. Platter, 12"l x 6"w.

PLATE 116.   DUNKELD, Frank Beardmore & Co., Mark 19B. Bread & Butter Plate, 7½"d.

PLATE 117. EAGLE, Podmore, Walker & Co., Mark 103a. Platter, 13½"l x 10½"w, pattern color is a very dark steel blue with Eagles almost black in color.

PLATE 118. EILEEN, W. H. Grindley, Mark 59. Soup Plate, 10"d.

PLATE 119. EXCELSIOR, Thomas Fell, Mark 50. Tea Pot with pedestal base.

PLATE 120. FAIRY VILLAS, unmarked, attributed to W. Adams & Co., see Plate 97 in FB1. Small Oval Dish, either for soap or individual serving dish, 5½"l x 4"w.

PLATE 121. FALLOW DEER, Wedgwood, similar to Mark 124a, with impressed "Wedgwood" marks and dating cyphers indicating circa 1885, similar to Mark 124. Plate, 10"d.

PLATE 122. FALLOW DEER, Wedgwood, similar to Marks 124 and 124a. Covered Serving Dish, square shape.

PLATE 123. FERRARA, Wedgwood, mark 124a. Pitcher, 6"h.

PLATE 124. FERRARA, Wedgwood, mark 124a. Plate, 10"d.

PLATE 125. FERRARA, Wedgwood, mark 124 (pattern identified for Plate 335 in FB1). Handleless Cup, 3"h.

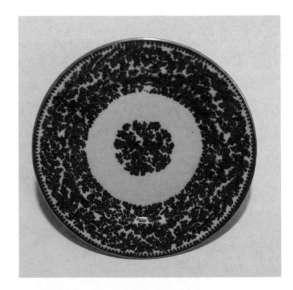

PLATE 126. FIBRE, Globe Pottery Company, circa 1917 (see Godden Mark 1711); additional printed mark indicating piece was made for Woolworth's. Plate, 6"d.

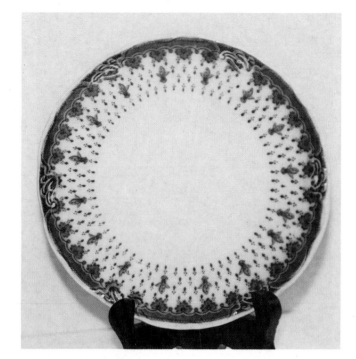

PLATE 127. FLEUR DE LIS, J. & G. Meakin, Mark 88. Saucer, 6"d.

PLATE 128. FLORAL, Thomas Hughes & Son, Mark 68a without pattern name (see Williams I, p. 178). Covered Vegetable Dish, rectangular size.

PLATE 129. FLORIAN, Burgess & Leigh, Mark 27 with a Registry Number circa 1909. Platter, oval, large size.

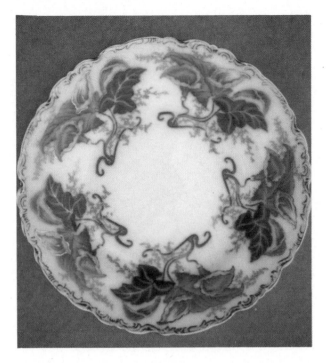

PLATE 130. FULTON, Johnson Bros., similar to Mark 71. Plate, 10"d.

PLATE 131. GENEVESE, Edge, Malkin & Co., Mark 48A. Plate, 9¼"d.

PLATE 132. GERANEUM, Podmore, Walker & Co., similar to initials in Mark 102. Plate, 9½"d.

PLATE 133. GIRONDE, W. H. Grindley, Mark 59. Berry Dish, 6"d.

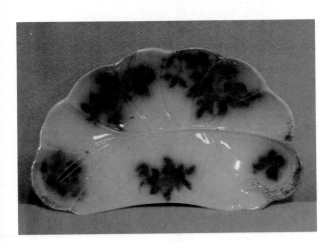

PLATE 134. GIRONDE, W. H. Grindley, Mark 59. Bone Dish.

PLATE 135. GIRONDE, W. H. Grindley, Mark 59 (pattern identified for Plate 341 in FB1; this pattern also is found with Mark 154). Cup, 2"h, and Saucer, 6"d.

PLATE 136. GLADIOLUS, Doulton, Mark 40a. Pitcher, 9"h.

PLATE 137. GRACE, W. H. Grindley, Mark 59. Plate, 9"d.

PLATE 139. GRECIAN SCROLL, T. J. & J. Mayer, circa mid 1800s. Pitcher, 6"h, figural bearded head spout, popularly called "North Wind" head.

PLATE 138. GRASSHOPPER AND FLOWERS, unmarked (Williams's pattern name, see Williams II, p. 43, attributed to Charles Meigh circa early 1840s). Milk Pitcher, 11"h, hinged metal lid, polychromed.

PLATE 140. GRECIAN STATUE, Brownfields Pottery, circa 1891-1900 (see Godden Mark 670). Drainer for Butter Dish.

PLATE 141. GREVILLE, Bishop & Stonier, Mark 20. Plate, 10¼"d.

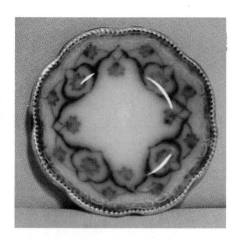

PLATE 142. HADDON, W. H. Grindley, Mark 59. This is the same pattern as Plate 411, Mark 157 (Libertas, Prussia) in FB1. Butter Pat.

PLATE 143. HADDON, W. H. Grindley, Mark 59. Platter, oval shape, 16¼"l x 11½"w.

PLATE 144. HAGUE, Josiah Wedgwood, Mark 124. Serving Tray, 17½"l x 8"w.

PLATE 145. HALFORD, Ford & Sons, Ltd., Mark 52a. Plate, 10"d.

PLATE 146. HANLEY, J. & G.
Meakin, Mark 89. Plate, 8½"d.

PLATE 147. HARVARD, Alfred Meakin, Ltd., Mark 86.
Plate, 10"d.

PLATE 148. HARVEST, Alfred
Meakin, Ltd., Mark 87; (unmarked pat-
tern name, see Williams II, p. 138).
Soup or Cereal Bowl 7⅞"d.

PLATE 149. HIZEN, Mason's, Mark 83C (unmarked
pattern name, see Plate 122 in FB1, attributed to Ashworth, successor to Mason's). Chamber Pot, 5½"h,
8½"d, handle formed in a snake shape.

PLATE 150. THE HOLLAND, Alfred Meakin, Ltd., Mark 86. Plate, 10"d, gold trim.

PLATE 151. HOMESTEAD, J. & G. Meakin, Mark 89. Saucer, 6"d.

PLATE 152. IDRIS, W. H. Grindley, Mark 61b in green. Platter, oval shape, 16"l x 11½"w.

PLATE 153. INDIAN, unidentified manufacturer, Mark 133. Saucer for Handleless Cup.

PLATE 154. INDIAN VASE, S. & E. H., unidentified manufacturer, Mark 112. Platter, 12½"l x 10"w.

PLATE 155. IRIS, Doulton, Mark 43 (correction for popular name for pattern in plate 332 in FB1). Cheese Dish, 9½"h x 9"d.

PLATE 156. IRIS, Arthur J. Wilkinson, Royal Staffordshire Pottery, Mark 125. Cup, 2¼"h x 3"d, and Saucer; pattern enhanced with gold outlining.

PLATE 157. IRIS, Arthur J. Wilkinson, Mark 125. Platter, oval shape, 13"l x 9½"w.

PLATE 158. IRIS, W. & E. Corn, Mark 35. Plate, 9"d; this example shows the pattern with a wide cobalt blue border which differs from the pattern shown in Plate 134 in FB1.

PLATE 159. IRIS, Mason's, Mark 83A; pattern name is not printed with mark, but the design is the same as the one made by Corn. Chamber Pot, 5½"h x 8½"d, gold trim and gold sponged work on body.

PLATE 160. IRIS, Cauldon, England, similar to name in Mark 29. Plate, 10"d, sponged gold work on body and around fluted border.

PLATE 161. ITALIA, unidentified manufacturer, Mark 116a. Saucer, 6"d.

PLATE 162. IVANHOE, Mark 22B, unidentified factory; this is not the same pattern as "Ivanhoe" made by Wedgwood (see Plate 136 in FB1). Miniature Cup, 2"h x 2"d, and Saucer, 4"d.

PLATE 163.   IVY (Williams's pattern name, see Williams I, p. 185), unmarked. Pitcher, 8"h, gold trim with gold pattern enhancement.

PLATE 164. IVY (same pattern as in preceding photograph), unmarked. Pitcher, 8"h.

PLATE 165. JANETTE, W. H. Grindley, Mark 59. Gravy Boat, 7½"l and Underplate, 8¾"l.

PLATE 166. JAPAN, T. Fell & Co., nineteenth century (exact mark not shown, see Mark 50). Tea Pot, pedestal base.

PLATE 167. JAPANESE, Minton & Hollins, Mark 94B. Soup Plate, 10½"d, polychromed pattern.

PLATE 168. JAPANESE, unmarked, border pattern only (see Williams I p. 32); Individual Salt, 1½"h x 2½"d, pedestal base.

PLATE 169. JEDO, Doulton, Mark 43a. Plate, 10"d.

PLATE 170. THOMAS JEFFERSON, Rowland & Marsellus, Mark 111a. Historical Commemorative Plate for the St. Louis World Fair.

PLATE 171. JEWEL, Johnson Bros., Mark 71. Set of graduated Pitchers.

PLATE 172.   KAOLIN, Podmore Walker & Co.,
Mark 102. Sugar Bowl with pedestal base.

PLATE 173. KENDAL, Ridgways, Mark 110. Plate,
10"d, gold trim on outer edge.

PLATE 174. KEW, Bourne & Leigh, Albion Pottery, Mark 22a. Platter, 14"l, oval shape.

PLATE 175. KISWICK, New Wharf Pottery, Mark 98. Platter, 14"l, oval shape.

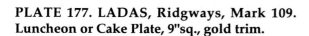

PLATE 176. LADAS, Ridgways, Mark 109. Gravy Boat and Underplate, 8¾"l, gold trim with gold outlining on embossed body designs.

PLATE 177. LADAS, Ridgways, Mark 109. Luncheon or Cake Plate, 9"sq., gold trim.

PLATE 178. LADAS, Ridgways, Mark 109. Covered Vegetable Dish, 9"l.

PLATE 179. LAKEWOOD, Wood & Son, Mark 131. Cup, 2"h and Saucer, 4"d; pattern is overlaid with gold designs.

PLATE 180. LE PAVOT, W. H. Grindley, Mark 59. Covered Vegetable Dish, 11"l x 7"d.

PLATE 181. LEIPSIC, J. Clementson, Mark 31A. Open Serving Dish, rectangular shape, 10½"l x 8"w.

PLATE 182. LILY, marked "Adderley" in blue, underglaze (see Williams II, p. 141, circa late 1800s). Pair of Vases, 9"h; gold tapestry work on base, neck, and handles combined with gold sponged work on body.

PLATE 183. LONSDALE, Samuel Ford & Co., Mark 50A. Gravy Boat, gold trim.

PLATE 184. LONSDALE, Samuel Ford & Co., Mark 50A. Covered Vegetable Dish and Tray, rectangular shapes, gold trim.

PLATE 185. LOTUS, unidentified manufacturer, Mark 28A. Jardiniere, gold spattered work around top of body.

PLATE 186. LOTUS, W. H. Grindley, Mark 61 (correction for manufacturer for Plate 167 in FB1). Open Vegetable Bowl, 10¼"l x 8"w.

PLATE 187. LOUISE, New Wharf Pottery, Mark 98. Oval Vegetable Bowl.

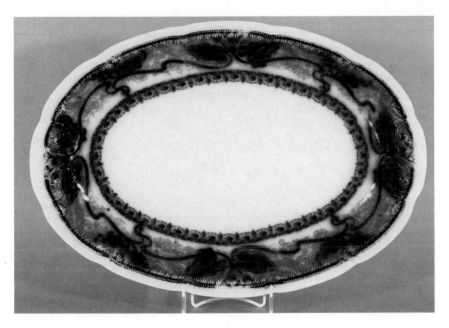

PLATE 188. MANSKILLAN, Wood & Sons, Mark 131. Platter, 16½"l x 11½"w, light gold work on center of leaves in pattern.

PLATE 189. MARECHAL NEIL, W. H. Grindley, Mark 59. Covered Sugar Bowl.

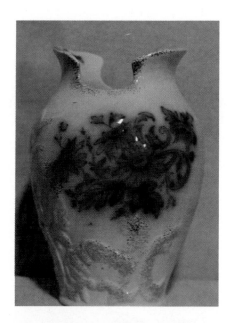

PLATE 191. MARGUERITE, H. Bros., Mark 62. Toothbrush Holder, gold sponged work on body.

PLATE 190. MARECHAL NEIL, W. H. Grindley, Mark 59. Fruit or Cereal Bowl, 6"d.

PLATE 193. MARTHA WASHINGTON, Josiah Wedgwood, Mark 124. Historical Commemorative Plate, 9"d.

PLATE 192. THE MARQUIS, W. H. Grindley, Mark 61b. Plate, 8"d. This photograph shows a clearer view of the gold trim on this pattern than Plate 184 in FB1.

PLATE 194. MEISSEN, T. Furnival, Mark 55a (impressed mark) with J. R. Gibney (importer) printed mark shown in Mark 55a. Fruit or Cereal Bowl.

PLATE 195. MELROSE, New Wharf Pottery, Mark 98. Soup Bowl, 9"d.

PLATE 196. MESSINA, Brown-Westhead, Moore, & Co., Mark 23 (correction for manufacturer for Plate 186 in FB1). Soup Bowl, 9"d.

PLATE 197. MESSINA, Alfred Meakin, Ltd., Mark 86. Covered Vegetable Dish.

PLATE 199. MONARCH, Myott, Son, & Co., Mark 97a. Pitcher, 5"h.

PLATE 198. MILAN, W. H. Grindley, Mark 59. Soup Tureen, 5"h x 7"l, with Ladle, gold trim.

PLATE 201. MONTANA, Johnson Bros., Mark 71. Plate, 10"d.

PLATE 200. MONGOLIAN, F. & W., Mark 49B, unidentified manufacturer. Plate, 10"d.

PLATE 202. MORNING GLORY, Thomas Hughes & Son, Mark 68a. Rose bowl, 6"d, gold trim.

PLATE 203. MORNING GLORY, unmarked (see Williams II, p. 147). Handleless Cup with pedestal base and Saucer.

PLATE 204. NAIDA, Upper Hanley Pottery, Mark 115. Plate, 6"d; this piece is also printed with an advertisement for "Crawford Cooking Ranges."

PLATE 205. NANKIN, unmarked, attributed to Cauldon, circa late 1800s (see Williams II, p. 53). Tea Pot, pedestal base.

PLATE 206. NANKIN, unmarked, attributed to Ashworth, circa mid 1860s (see Williams I, p. 194). Pitcher without spout 4¼"h.

PLATE 207. NANKIN, Doulton, Mark 42. Plate, 10½"d.

PLATE 208. NAVARRE, Wedgwood & Co., Ltd., Mark 121a. Saucer, 6½"d, pattern enhanced with gold.

PLATE 209. NEOPOLITAN, Johnson Bros., Mark 70. Saucer, 6"d, gold designs superimposed over printed Flow Blue pattern.

PLATE 210. NON PAREIL, Burgess & Leigh, Mark 25. Saucer or Underplate (extended shape forms rest for spoon or ladle).

PLATE 211. NORAH, T. Rathbone & Co., Mark 105. Plate, 8"d, gold trim.

PLATE 212. NORFOLK, Doulton, Mark 43. Bowl, 8"d; this example does not have the pictorial inner border pattern shown in the following examples.

PLATE 213. NORFOLK, Doulton, Mark 43. Soup or Cereal Bowl with pictorial inner border.

PLATE 214. NORFOLK, Doulton, Mark 43. Plate, 10"d.

PLATE 215. NORFOLK, Doulton, Mark 43. Saucer for Cup in following photograph.

PLATE 216. NORFOLK, Doulton, Mark 43. Cup, variation of center scene showing buildings as well as windmill.

PLATE 217. OAKLAND, John Maddock and Sons, Mark 83. Butter Pat, 2¾" x 2⅞".

PLATE 218. OCEAN, unidentified manufacturer, Mark 138. Saucer, 6"d, semi-nude figures bathing in ocean.

PLATE 219. OLD CASTLES, Henry Alcock & Co., Mark 11a in green with pattern name printed in separate blue mark with a registry date circa 1913. Plate, 10"d.

PLATE 220. OLD CURIOSITY SHOP, Ridgways, circa early 1900s, with "Humphries Clock" trademark (see Williams II, p. 100). Serving Pieces from a child's set of china are shown in this and the following three photographs. (The complete set for 6 also included Dinner Plates, 4½"d; Luncheon Plates, 3⅞"d; Open Vegetable Bowl, 4"l x 4"w.) Soup Bowl, 4⅜"d.

PLATE 221. OLD CURIOSITY SHOP, Platter, 8¼"l x 6½"w.

PLATE 222. OLD CURIOSITY SHOP, Platter, 6⅛"l x 4¾"w. Two other Platters (not shown) are included in set (7⅛"l x 5⅝"w and 5⅛"l x 4"w).

PLATE 223. OLD CURIOSITY SHOP, Covered Soup Tureen, 4⅛"h x 6⅞"d (back left); Covered Sauce Tureen, 3"h x 4⅝"l (back right) with Ladle, 3½"l; Covered Vegetable Dish, 3⅜"h x 5⅞"l (front center).

PLATE 224. OLD ENGLISH RURAL SCENES, William Adams & Sons, Mark 7a (the third word in the pattern name is not clear, but it appears to be "Rural" and fits the pattern portrayed, Plate, 10"d.

PLATE 225. ONION, Allertons, Mark 16. Plate, 8"d.

PLATE 226. OREGON, T. J. & J. Mayer, similar to Mark 84. Sugar Bowl with pedestal base (handle missing from this example).

PLATE 227. OREGON, T. J. & J. Mayer, similar to Mark 84. Tea Pot with pedestal base.

PLATE 228. OREGON, Johnson Bros., Mark 71. Cup, 2⅜"h, Saucer, 6"d; gold trim and pattern enhanced with gold.

PLATE 230. OREGON, Johnson Bros., Mark 71. Covered Vegetable Dish, oval shape, 11½"l x 9½"d, scalloped footed base.

PLATE 229. OREGON, Johnson Bros., Mark 71. Plate, 8¾"d.

PLATE 231. ORIENTAL, Samuel Alcock, Mark 14a (correction for Mark 79 in FB1 and Plate 213 in FB1). Sauce Tureen, polychromed on outer rim of lid, gold trim and gold highlights on pattern.

PLATE 232. ORIENTAL, Samuel Alcock, Mark 14a. Plate, 10½"d.

PLATE 233. ORIENTAL, New Wharf Pottery, Mark 100a. Plate, 10"d (close up view of pattern).

PLATE 234. ORLEANS, Thomas Dimmock, Mark 39a (correction for manufacturer in Plate 214 in FB1). Platter, 16"l x 14"w.

PLATE 235. ORMONDE, Alfred Meakin, Ltd., Mark 86. Covered Waste Jar, 13½"h.

PLATE 236. ORMONDE, Alfred Meakin, Ltd., Mark 86. Wash Bowl, 5½"h x 16¾"w; Pitcher, 13¼"h.

PLATE 237. ORMONDE, Alfred Meakin, Ltd., Mark 86. Pieces from a Wash Set: Shaving Mug, 4¼"h; Covered Soap Dish, 4½"l x 5½"w; Toothbrush Holder, 5¾"h; Hot Water Pitcher, 6½"h.

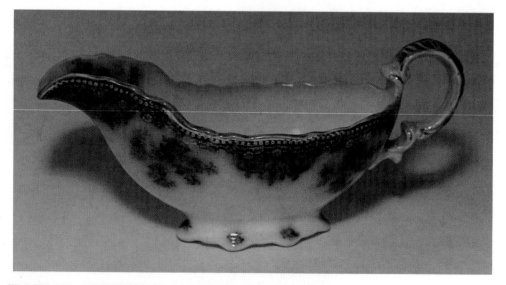

PLATE 238. OSBORNE, W. H. Grindley, Mark 60. Gravy Boat, 6½"l, gold trim.

PLATE 239. OSBORNE, Ridgways, Mark 109. Gravy Boat, 6½"l, gold trim.

PLATE 240. OYAMA, Doulton, Mark 44a. Pitcher, 6½"h.

PLATE 241. PANSY, unmarked, attributed to Johnson Bros., circa early 1900s (see Williams II, p. 150). Pitcher, 9"h, gold trim and outlining on pattern.

PLATE 242. PEACH, Johnson Bros., Mark 70. Platter, 17"l x 14"w.

PLATE 243. PEKIN, Arthur J. Wilkinson, Royal Staffordshire Pottery, Mark 126a. Plate, 8"d; note this example only has the border pattern of Pekin (see Williams I, p. 44 for the center pattern).

PLATE 244. PEKIN, unidentified manufacturer, "Pat. Oct. 21/02" appears with pattern name. Plate with Cup and Saucer.

PLATE 245. PEKIN, Davenport, Mark 37a. Plate, 10½"d, pattern accented with gold.

PLATE 246. PEKIN, Thomas Dimmock, Mark 39a. Plate, 8"d; Handleless Cup, 2¾"h x 3⅝"d, and Cup Plate, 1⅛"h x 5¾"d.

PLATE 247. PEKIN, unmarked, except for Registry Number 538202 (circa 1908); attributed to Albert Jones, (see Plate 226 in FB1). Covered Vegetable Dish, 6½"h x 12"l x 8"w, scalloped footed base.

PLATE 248. PEMBROKE, Bishop & Stonier, Mark 20. Soup Plate, 10"d.

PLATE 249. PENANG, William Ridgway, oriental style mark with name, circa early 1830s. Platter, 16"l x 12"w, rectangular shape.

PLATE 250. PERSIAN SPRAY, Doulton, Mark 43. Cake Stand, 3"h x 9"d, pattern overlaid with gold designs.

PLATE 251. PETUNIA, manufacturer not identified; the mark is like Mark 62, except it has the initials "C. & H." rather than "H. Bros." Jardiniere, 6½"h x 8½"d; pattern enhanced with gold.

PLATE 252. POPPY, W. H. Grindley, Mark 60. Soup Tureen, 5"h x 13"l with Platter, 14"l x 10"w; gold outlining on pattern with gold sponged work on handles and finial.

PLATE 253. POPPY, Doulton, Mark 44. Set of 3 graduated Pitchers: 7¾"h (center); 6⅝"h (right); and 5¾"h (left).

PLATE 254. POPPY, New Wharf Pottery, Mark 99. Plate, 8¾"d.

PLATE 255. POPPY, unmarked pattern (Williams's pattern name, see Williams II, p. 196), W. Adams & Co. Mark (not shown) with a registration mark circa 1881. Bowl, 10"d.

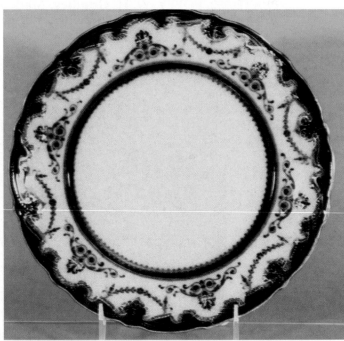

PLATE 256. PORTMAN, W. H. Grindley, Mark 60. Plate, 9"d.

PLATE 257. PORTSMOUTH, New Wharf Pottery, Mark 98. Plate, 9"d, gold work around outer border.

PLATE 258. PRINCETON, Johnson Bros., Mark 70. Butter Pat.

PLATE 259. QUEEN ALEXANDRA and KING EDWARD VII, unmarked. Historical Commemorative Cake Plate, 8½"d, polychromed portraits and wide cobalt blue border.

PLATE 260. REBECCA (Williams's pattern name, see Williams I, p. 197), George Jones & Sons (see Kovel Mark 79F; also marked with a Lion mark with "England"). Plate, 8½"d.

PLATE 261. REGENT, unidentified manufacturer; pattern name is printed within a wreath shape with "England," circa after 1891. Plate, 9"d.

PLATE 262. RETURN OF THE MAYFLOWER, Wedgwood & Co. impressed mark (not shown), after 1860. Historical Commemorative Plate, 9½"d.

PLATE 263. PAUL REVERE (RIDE OF), Rowland & Marsellus, Mark 111a. Historical Commemorative Plate, 10"d.

PLATE 264. RHINE, Thomas Dimmock, Mark 39. Underplate for Sauce Tureen shown in the following photographs.

PLATE 265. RHINE, Sauce Tureen and Ladle.

PLATE 266. RHINE, interior of Sauce Tureen shown in preceding photograph.

PLATE 267. RHODA GARDENS, Hackwood, Mark 62A. Plate, 9½"d.

PLATE 268. RHONE, Thomas Furnival & Co., similar to Mark 54. Tea Pot with pedestal base (lid missing).

PLATE 269. RHONE, unmarked pattern name with illegible impressed mark; pattern is the same as the one by Furnival shown in the preceding photographs. Pitcher, 6½"h.

PLATE 270. RICHMOND, unmarked (see Williams III, p. 58, Ford & Sons, similar to Mark 51a shown in Marks Section). Platter, 12¼"l x 10"d, rectangular shape.

PLATE 272. ROMANCE, unmarked (Williams's pattern name, see Williams II, p. 103). Jam or Honey Dish, 5"d.

PLATE 271. ROCK, E. Challinor, Mark 30a. Saucer.

PLATE 273. ROSE, W. H. Grindley, Mark 60. Gravy Boat with Underplate, gold trim.

PLATE 274. ROSES AND RIBBONS, John Maddock and Sons, Mark 83. Berry Dish, 7½"d and Drainer, 8¾"d, gold trim with gold sponged work on body.

PLATE 275. ROSEVILLE, John Maddock and Sons, Mark 83. Compote, 4"h x 9"d, gold trim.

PLATE 276. ROSEVILLE, John Maddock and Sons, Mark 83. Platter 14½"l x 10"w.

PLATE 277. ROSLYN, Alfred Colley, Ltd., Mark 33a. Plate, 10"d.

PLATE 278. SALISBURY, Ford & Sons, Mark 51a. Wash Bowl and Pitcher showing exterior view of Bowl.

PLATE 279. SALISBURY, Pitcher, 12"h, to Wash Set.

PLATE 280. SALISBURY, Bowl, 16"d, to Wash Set showing interior decoration.

PLATE 281. SATSUMA, Brown-Westhead, Moore, & Co., Mark 23. Covered Serving Dish on footed stand, 5"h x 12"d (ribbon shaped finial is broken on this example).

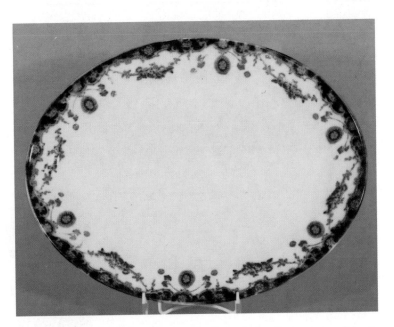

PLATE 282. SAVOY, Empire Porcelain Company, Mark 49A. Platter, 13½"l x 10½"w, oval shape.

PLATE 283. SCINDE, unmarked (same pattern as made by J. & G. Alcock, see Plate 254 in FB1). Tureen on pedestal base, 7½"h x 9"l.

PLATE 284. SCINDE, J. & G. Alcock, Mark 13. Covered Soap Dish (only the floral border part of the Scinde pattern decorates this piece).

PLATE 285. SCINDE, T. Walker, circa mid 1800s; mark (not shown) consists of "T. Walker" over "Ironstone" and pattern name. Platter, 12¼"l x 9½"w, rectangular shape.

PLATE 286. SHANGHAE, J. Furnival & Co., Mark 53A. Relish or one handled Serving Dish.

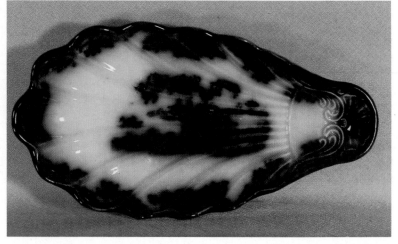
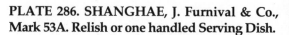

PLATE 287. SHANGHAE, J. Furnival & Co., Mark 53A. Sugar Bowl with pedestal base (lid missing).

PLATE 288. SHANGHAE, J. Furnival & Co. Cover to Vegetable Dish.

PLATE 289. SHANGHAI, unidentified manufacturer, Mark 116. Cup and Saucer.

PLATE 290. SHANGHAI, W. Adams, Mark 2a. Plate, 9¼"d, paneled shape.

PLATE 291. SHAPOO, T. & R. Boote, Mark 20A. Plate, 10"d.

PLATE 292. SHAPOO, unmarked, pattern is the same as shown in preceding photograph. Pitcher, 8"h.

PLATE 293. SHELL, E. Challinor, similar to Mark 30a. Tea Pot with pedestal base.

PLATE 294. SIMLA, marked "Imported by E. M. Forster & Co." without pattern name (see Williams I, p. 50 and Plate 263 in FB1). Plate, 10"d.

PLATE 295. SINGAN, attributed to Thomas Goodfellow, circa mid 1840s (see Williams III, p. 62). Handleless Cup with pedestal base.

PLATE 296. SIVA, manufacturer mark illegible. Platter, oval shape, large size, polychromed.

PLATE 297. SPIRIT OF '76, marked "Ye Olde Historical Pottery," manufacturer not identified. Historical Commemorative Plate, 9"d.

PLATE 298. SPODE'S TOWER, W. T. Copeland, Mark 33B. Platter.

PLATE 300. SPODE'S TOWER, pieces from Tea Set shown in preceding photograph: Covered Sugar Bowl, Creamer, Tea Pot, and Cup and Saucer.

PLATE 299. SPODE'S TOWER, W. T. Copeland, variation of Mark 33B, circa early 1920s. Tea Plate, Cream Pitchers, and Cup.

PLATE 302. STANLEY, Johnson Bros., Mark 71. Gravy Boat, 8"l with underplate 8"l.

PLATE 301. STANLEY, Johnson Bros., Mark 72. Saucer, 6½"d, pattern enhanced with gold.

PLATE 303. STANLEY, Johnson Bros.,
Mark 71. Covered Butter Dish, 4¼"h x 8"d.

PLATE 304. STANLEY, Johnson Bros.,
Mark 71. Covered Sugar Bowl, 5"h, and
Creamer, 5¾"h.

PLATE 305. STRATFORD,
Burgess & Leigh, Middle-
port Pottery, Mark 24.
Shaving Mug, 4¼"h; Water
Pitcher, 12"h; Pitcher, 7½"h;
gold embellishes part of
pattern.

PLATE 306. SUTTON, Ridgways, Mark 110.
Plate, 9"d, gold outlining on parts of floral
design.

PLATE 307. SWALLOW, Grove & Stark, Mark 61A. Plate, 10"d.

PLATE 308. SYDNEY, New Wharf Pottery, similar to Mark 98. Saucer, 5¾"d, gold trim.

PLATE 309. THE TEMPEST, Doulton, Mark 43; pattern is from Doulton's Shakespeare Series. Irregular shaped dish, 8"x 6".

PLATE 310. THE TEMPLE, Podmore, Walker & Co., Mark 103a. Handleless Cup, 3"h, and Saucer, 6"d.

PLATE 311. THISTLE, manufacturer mark illegible. Vase with gold trim on neck and base and gold sponged work on body.

PLATE 312. TIVOLI, T. Furnival & Co., similar to Mark 54. Platter, 15"l x 13"w, rectangular shape. This platter was also made in a 41"l x 33"w size.

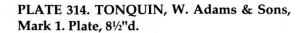

PLATE 313. TIVOLI, unmarked; pattern is the same as the one by T. Furnival shown in the preceding photograph. Sauce Tureen with Underplate and Ladle.

PLATE 314. TONQUIN, W. Adams & Sons, Mark 1. Plate, 8½"d.

PLATE 315. TONQUIN, W. Adams & Sons, Mark 1. Rectangular shaped Fruit or Serving Dish on short pedestal base, 12¼"l x 9⅞"w.

PLATE 316. TOWER, unmarked (Williams's pattern name, see Williams II, p. 107; pattern name noted for Plate 357 in FB1). Plate, 10"d.

PLATE 317. TRENT, Bishop & Stonier, Mark 20a. Set of graduated Pitchers: 7¼"h; 8"h; 9"h; pattern enhanced with gold outlining.

PLATE 318. TURKEY, unmarked. Plate, 9½"d.

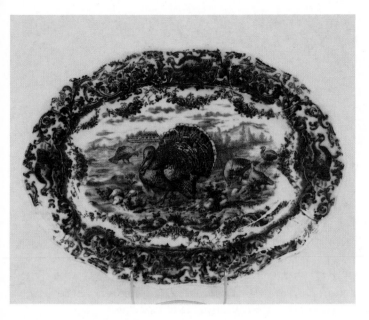

PLATE 319. TURKEY, unmarked. Platter, oval shape, 18"l x 13½"w.

PLATE 320. TURKEY/WILD TURKEY (popular name), "Cauldon England" printed in blue, similar to printed name in Mark 29. Platter, 23¼"l x 19½"w, rectangular shape.

PLATE 321. TYNE, Bridgwood & Son, Mark 22A. Saucer, 5½"d.

PLATE 322. UNITED STATES CAPITOL, Arthur J. Wilkinson, Royal Staffordshire Pottery, Mark 125. Historical Scenic Plate, 8½"d.

PLATE 323. VANE, Alfred Meakin, Ltd., Mark 86. Butter Pat, 3⅛"d, gold outer border and floral design accented in gold.

PLATE 324. VENTNOR, manufacturer unidentified, pattern name printed in fancy scrolled design with "England," circa after 1891. Platter, 16⅜"l x 12"w.

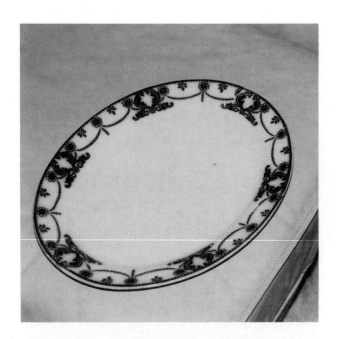

PLATE 325. VENUS, Till & Sons, Mark 114. Large oval shaped Platter.

PLATE 326. VERMONT, Burgess & Leigh, Mark 26. Soup Tureen, gold trim.

PLATE 328. VERONA, Wood & Son, Mark 131. Pitcher, 8½"h.

PLATE 327. VERONA, Ford & Sons, Ltd., Mark 52. Plate, 9¾"d.

PLATE 330. WARWICK, unmarked, attributed to Podmore, Walker & Co., (see Williams II, p. 110). Tea Pot, 8¼"h, pedestal base.

PLATE 329. WALDORF, New Wharf Pottery, Mark 98. Bowl, 3"h x 9"d.

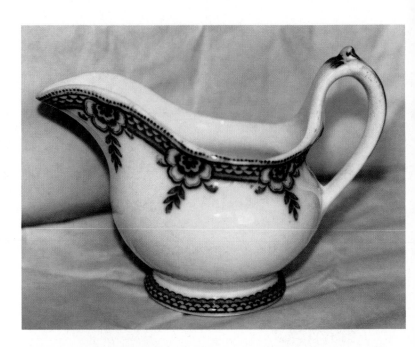

PLATE 332. WATFORD, Ford & Sons, Ltd., Mark 52a. Gravy Boat.

PLATE 331. WATER NYMPH, unmarked, same pattern as made by Josiah Wedgwood, circa early 1870s (see Williams II, p. 166). Pitcher, 10½"h.

PLATE 333. WATTEAU, Doulton, Mark 41a. Plate, 10"d, only the border design of the pattern is on this piece.

PLATE 334. WATTEAU, Doulton, Mark 43. Saucer, 5½"d, full pattern.

PLATE 335. WAVERLY, John Maddock, Mark 83. Saucer, 6"d, pattern enhanced with gold.

PLATE 336. WELLINGTON, J. & G. Meakin, similar to Mark 88. Wash Bowl, 5¼"h x 16¾"w; Pitcher, 11¾"h; gold trim and pattern embellished with gold.

PLATE 337. WELLINGTON, Chamber Pot with Lid.

PLATE 338. WELLINGTON, accessory pieces from Wash Set: Shaving Mug, 3¾"h; Toothbrush Holder, 5½"h; Covered Soap Dish, 3½"h x 5½"w; Hot Water Pitcher, 7½"h.

PLATE 339. WHAMPOA, unmarked, attributed to Mellor, Venables, & Co., circa 1830s (see Williams I, p. 56 and II, p. 75). Pitcher, 7¼"h.

PLATE 340. WHAMPOA (this pattern appears to match the "Whampoa" example made by the Cambrian Pottery in Swansea, Wales as shown in Williams I, p. 75; she notes that "the high-prowed boat and island at top right" are not part of this pattern, circa mid 1800s). Saucer, 6"d.

PLATE 341. WILLOW, Doulton (mark not shown), circa late 1800s. Mixing Bowls, 9"d and 7"d.

PLATE 343. WILLOW, unmarked. Pitcher, 6"h, pattern accented with gold and gold trim.

PLATE 342. WILLOW (pattern name unmarked), C. T. Maling, Cetem Ware, Mark 83B. Lamp Base.

PLATE 344. WILLOW, unmarked. Tea Pot, 7"h (same mold as Pitcher in preceding photograph).

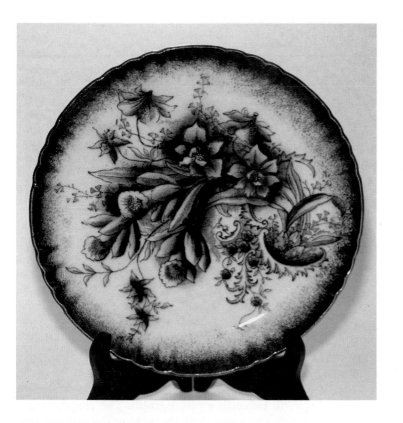

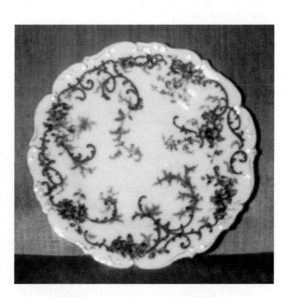

PLATE 346. YORK (Williams's pattern name, see Williams III, p. 60), marked "Cauldon, England" and "Pitkin & Brooks, Chicago." Plate, 9"d.

PLATE 345. WINDSOR, C. T. Maling, Mark 83A. Plate, 9"d, gold trim on outer rim with enamelled work on interior of floral designs.

Unidentified English Patterns

PLATE 348. Tea Set: Tea Pot, 4½"h, with Covered Sugar and Creamer, scalloped pedestal base, Brown-Westhead, Moore & Co., similar to Mark 23; blue floral branches scattered over body, gold trim.

PLATE 347. Wall Plate, 11¼"d, Bishop & Stonier "Bisto," Mark 20; light to dark blue floral design covers surface.

PLATE 349. Wash Bowl, 6"h x 15¾"d, marked "Cauldon, England" (see printed part of mark 29); non-historical scenic decor.

PLATE 350. Pitcher, 11½"h, for Bowl shown in preceding photograph. The floral border is the same, but the scenic decoration features cattle.

PLATE 351. Sauce Tureen, 6¼"h, and Underplate, 8"d, W. T. Copeland, circa 1891; Oriental style floral pattern.

PLATE 352. Pitcher, 7¾"h, Doulton, Mark 42; large blue flowers and small leaves cover body on white background with solid cobalt blue borders and handle.

PLATE 353. Cheese Dish, 7½"h x 11½"l, Doulton, Mark 44; mixed flowers form pattern, gold trim.

PLATE 354. Gravy Boat, marked "Parisian Granite, Thomas Elsmore & Son, England," with a registry mark circa 1878; Oriental style floral design featuring a vase with flowers.

PLATE 355. Loving Cup, 5"h, Empire Porcelain Company, Stoke-on-Trent, England (mark not shown), circa 1940s; floral and leaf pattern highlighted in gold; dark cobalt blue borders and handles.

PLATE 356. Jardiniere, 9⅜"h x 8½"d, footed base, Thomas Forester & Sons, Mark 52A; pattern composed of large open petaled flowers.

PLATE 357. Vegetable Bowl, 10"d, J. Kent, Mark 79 (manufacturer identified for Plate 373 in FB1; this example carries factory mark); non-historical scenic design featuring a large palace type structure with figures in the foreground.

PLATE 358. Vegetable Bowl, 10¼"d, J. Kent, Mark 79. This example shows the same decoration as the one in the preceding photograph, but the mold is different.

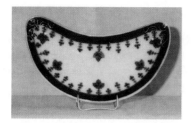

PLATE 359. Bone Dish, marked "J. & G. Meakin," circa late 1800s; stylized floral design around inner border.

PLATE 360. Cup and Saucer, marked "J. & G. Meakin," circa late 1800s; floral vine pattern around inner border.

PLATE 361. Butter Pat, 3⅛"d, Alfred Meakin, Ltd., Mark 87; floral center and border pattern.

PLATE 362. Platter, 12¼"l x 9½"w, J. & G. Meakin, Mark 88; Oriental style floral design with small buildings in the background.

PLATE 363. Wall Plaque or Charger, 11⅝"d, J. & G. Meakin, Mark 89; non-historical scenic decor of a house at the foot of mountains with a figure in the foreground; embossed designs around outer border are outlined in gold.

PLATE 364. Plate, 8"d, William Ridgway, impressed initials with "Opaque Granite China," circa early 1830s geometric design composed of star shapes scattered around inner border with one in the center.

PLATE 365. Platter, Ridgways, Mark 110 without "England"; Oriental style floral border with undecorated center.

PLATE 366. Pitcher, 6¾"h, Josiah Wedgwood, Mark 124 with year cyphers for December 1871; floral design covers body with a wide yellow-brown center band decorated with stylized geometric designs.

PLATE 367. Platter, 17"l x 12"w, illegible mark; Oriental style peacock decorates center.

PLATE 368. Plate, 9½"d, unidentified manufacturer, see Mark 100A; this pattern is similar to Persian Spray, but it is not the same. (See Persian Spray, photograph 250.)

PLATE 369. Vase, 14"h, mark illegible, except for "England"; non-historical scenic decor featuring a cottage and a lake.

Unidentified Patterns and Manufacturers

PLATE 370. Butter Pat, 3"d, wide cobalt blue border featuring a blue and white abstract design, unmarked.

PLATE 371. Plate, 10"d, attached to metal warming pan; wide floral border pattern, unmarked.

PLATE 372. Plate, 7¾"d, shaggy petaled floral sprays scattered over body, gold trim, unmarked.

PLATE 373. Cup Plate, scroll work composes border and center pattern. (The border pattern appears to be the same as that used on Columbia, see Williams I, p. 62.)

PLATE 374. Bread Plate, 10¼"d, large flowers decorate center and extend toward outer border, unmarked.

PLATE 375. Bowl, 10"d, large lily and leaf center pattern with solid cobalt blue outer border, gold trim, unmarked.

PLATE 376. Tea Cup, 2½"h x 4¼"d, and Saucer, Oriental style floral pattern composes border and center decor. The following five pictures show other pieces in this pattern; unmarked.

PLATE 377. Demi-Tasse Cup and Saucer.

PLATE 378. Waste Bowl for Tea Set.

PLATE 379. Covered Sugar Bowl and Creamer, scalloped pedestal base.

PLATE 380. Cake or Sandwich Plate, 8¼"d.

PLATE 381. Cake or Sandwich Plate, 10¾" x 9".

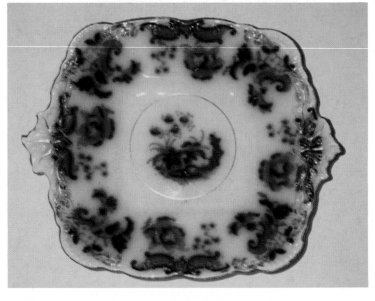

PLATE 382. Butter Pat, clusters of roses form a random design over body, unmarked.

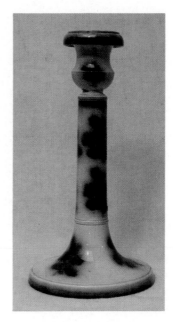

PLATE 383. Candle Holder, 12"h, floral pattern, unmarked.

PLATE 384. Clock, 2"h x 4¼"d, designed for desk or dresser; sailboats decorate two reserves around body, unmarked.

PLATE 385. Cup and Saucer, abstract geometric designs form pattern, unmarked.

PLATE 386. Dresser Set: Tray, 19½"l x 7½"w; pair of Candle Holders, 6½"h; two Covered Boxes, 3"h; one Covered Box, 3½"h; Pin Tray, 3½"x 2¾"; Ring Tree, 3"h x 4½"l; floral clusters form pattern, unmarked.

PLATE 387. Dresser Tray from set in preceding photograph showing center pattern.

PLATE 388. Jardiniere, 13½"h x 15½"d, large cobalt blue floral clusters scattered over body with gold sponged work around neck, unmarked.

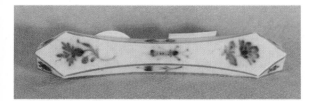

PLATE 389. Knife Rest, six sided, 4"l, bee and flower pattern, gold trim, unmarked.

PLATE 390. Ladle, wide floral border pattern on bowl of ladle with same decoration on handle, gold luster trim, unmarked.

PLATE 392. Mustard Pot, 3¾"h, metal hinged lid, floral pattern on body and neck, unmarked.

PLATE 391. Cup, 2¼"h, scroll work and fleurs de lis form wide border pattern, unmarked.

PLATE 393. Creamer, 2½"h x 2"l; pattern composed of flowers and scrolled work, unmarked.

PLATE 394. Creamer, cobalt blue flowers with gold dots forming centers; gold sponged work on body, unmarked.

PLATE 395. Pitcher, 4½"h, Oriental scenic decor of fisherman crossing bridge, unmarked.

PLATE 396. Pitcher, 8¼"h, Oriental scenic decor featuring two figures and a large umbrella, unmarked.

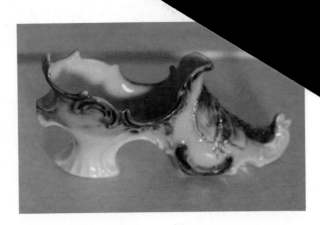

PLATE 398. Shoe, 3¼"h x 6¾"l, novelty or souvenir item, unmarked.

PLATE 397. Pitcher, 8"h, large flowers decorate body with pattern enhanced by gold spattered work, unmarked.

PLATE 399. Vase, 4½"h, four sides: one panel decorated with a sailboat; two sides decorated with a floral design; one side undecorated; unmarked.

PLATE 400. Vase showing floral decorated panels.

❧ 153 ❧

PLATE 401. Chamber Pot, 5¾"h x 10"d, raised flowers and leaves decorate body with raised scrolled work around border; gold trim and gold sponged work accents pattern, unmarked.

PLATE 402. Wash Set: Bowl, 19"d; Pitcher, 13"h; floral pattern covers most of body, gold lustre trim, unmarked.

PLATE 403. Wash Set: Bowl, 16"d; Pitcher, 12"h, Art Nouveau style floral pattern, unmarked.

Handpainted Flow Blue

PLATE 404. Plate, 10½"d, "Aster & Grapeshot," attributed to Clementson, circa 1840s (see Williams III, p. 64).

PLATE 405. Plate, 9½"d, "Bluebell & Grapes with Cherry Border" (see Williams II, p. 216).

PLATE 406. Plate, 10½"d, "Gingham Flower," unmarked.

PLATE 407. Handleless Cup and Saucer, "Heath's Flower," attributed to T. Heath, circa early 1830s (see Williams I, p. 182).

PLATE 409. Waste Bowl, 2½"h x 5"d, Lion and Crown mark, unidentified manufacturer, possible non-English.

PLATE 408. Plate, 9"d, "Leaf and Worm," unmarked.

PLATE 410. Handleless cup, 2½"h x 3¾"d, unmarked.

PLATE 411. Cup and Saucer, porcelain body, probably non-English, unmarked.

PLATE 412. Creamer, 3"h, "Crossed Bands" or "Crossed Swords," with copper lustre added to design, unmarked.

PLATE 413. Pepper Shaker and Mustard Pot, 3"h, hand-painted design with copper lustre, unmarked.

PLATE 414. Cup and Saucer, "Dahlia," with copper lustre, Charles Allerton & Sons, Mark 15.

PLATE 415. Handleless Cup and Saucer, "Lustre Band," attributed to Elsmore & Forster (see Williams II, p. 222, circa 1860s).

PLATE 416. Shaving Mug, polychromed floral pattern with copper lustre, unmarked.

PLATE 417. Handleless Cups: left, "Grape" pattern with copper lustre; center, "Wild Rose," polychromed; right, large flower with leaves, polychromed; unmarked.

PLATE 418. Pitcher, 5½"h, geometric and floral pattern, polychromed, unmarked.

PLATE 419. Reverse of Pitcher in preceding photograph decorated with a bird and leaf pattern.

PLATE 420. Pitcher, 7½"h, with hinged pewter lid, large floral and leaf pattern (combination of transfer and handpainted work), polychromed, unmarked.

Non-English Flow Blue

PLATE 421. UTOPIA, Crescent Pottery, Trenton, New Jersey, Mark 161A. Plate, 9"d; American.

PLATE 422. WINONA, illegible factory mark; pattern name is stamped on this example, and it is the same pattern as one made by The French China Co. in the following two photographs. Pitcher, 5"h; American.

PLATE 423. WINONA, The French China Co., "La Francaise," similar to Mark 163. Bread & Butter Plate, 6"d. ("La Francaise" is not the pattern name. It is a mark designating the factory.) American.

PLATE 424. WINONA, The French China Co., similar to Mark 163. Cup and Saucer; American.

PLATE 425. Plate 10"d, unmarked, attributed to The French China Co., fruit decor; (see other examples with similar border patterns); American.

PLATE 426. Cup and Saucer, unmarked, attributed to The French China Co., fruit decor.

PLATE 427. Plate, 7"d, octagonal shape, fruit decor, The French China Co., Mark 163; American.

PLATE 428. Plate, 10"d, The French China Co., Mark 162; white roses with multi-colored leaves and a wide cobalt blue border; American.

PLATE 429. PILGRIMS LANDING, The French China Co. Oval shaped Bowl decorated with historical scenic decor of Pilgrims kneeling and praying; American.

PLATE 430. Plate made by The French China Co; decorated with ship approaching land, part of the PILGRIMS LANDING historical scenes. Another view (not shown) is of Pilgrims waving from shore; American.

PLATE 431. Bowl, 9¾"d, marked "Imperial China Co.," a mark used by the Pioneer Pottery of Wellsville, Ohio, circa 1885 to 1896 (see Lehner, 1988; 349); red raspberries decorate center with wide cobalt blue border and gold trim; American.

PLATE 432. Vase, 11"h, reclining Tiger decorates center with wide cobalt blue borders at neck and base; made by Knowles, Taylor, Knowles, East Liverpool, Ohio, circa early 1900s (mark not show); American.

PLATE 434. LUZERNE, Mercer Pottery Company, see Mark 166. Ladle, gold trim; American.

PLATE 433. PAISLEY, Mercer Pottery Company, Trenton, New Jersey, Mark 166. Plate, 8"d; American.

PLATE 435. Platter, TURKEY decor, marked "Oliver China," (mark not shown), Sebring, Ohio, circa early 1900s; American.

PLATE 436. Plates, 9½"d, unmarked (correction for origin of this pattern shown in Plate 356 in FB1); American, matches pattern in preceding photograph.

PLATE 437. Cake Plate, 11½"sq, bell shaped flowers, gold trim; Sebring Pottery Company, Sebring, Ohio, Mark 166A; American.

PLATE 438. Cup, 2½"h, marked "Sterling China" with a crown, attributed to The Sterling China Company of Ohio, circa ealry 1900s (manufacturer identified for Plate 340 in FB1); American. (Note that "Sterling" is the name of the manufacturer, it is not a pattern name.)

PLATE 440. PANSY, Warwick China Co. Cake Plate, 10"d, gold trim; American, circa early 1900s.

PLATE 439. Butter Pat, 3½"h, unmarked, same pattern as Cup in preceding photograph; American.

PLATE 441. Bowl, 10"d, Warwick China Co., small floral pattern covers body, gold trim; American.

PLATE 442. Jardiniere, 7½"h x 8"d, Warwick China Co., marbled pattern, gold trim; American.

PLATE 443. LA BELLE, unmarked, attributed to Wheeling Pottery Co., Wheeling, West Virginia, see Marks 167 and 168. Biscuit Jar, 7"h; American.

PLATE 444. Fish Platter, 21"l x 9"w, unmarked; American.

PLATE 445. Souvenir Plate, 8¼"d, unmarked, decorated with colored transfer scene of the Panama Canal; American.

PLATE 446. Pitcher, 10"h, unmarked, probably American or European origin; figural decor of a monk drinking wine and carrying a food basket; pewter rim and spout.

PLATE 447. Reverse side of Pitcher in preceding photograph showing window of a wine cellar.

PLATE 449. Tom & Jerry Bowl, 5¼" h x 13"w (punch bowl), Keller & Guerin, similar to Mark 145; French.

PLATE 448. EGLANTINE, Keller & Guerin, Mark 145. Cup and Saucer; French.

PLATE 450. PARAPETTE, Keller & Guerin, Mark 145. Cup and Saucer; French.

PLATE 451. Plate, 8"d, marked "Opaque, Luneville, France" with a shield (similar to Mark 146, Utzchneider & Co.). Note that "Opaque" is not the pattern name; French.

PLATE 452. Oval Bowl, 13"l x 11"w, manufacturer unidentified, attributed to French origin; Boy and Calf figural decor.

PLATE 453. Hair Receiver, 4½" x 2½", Reinhold Schlegelmilch Co., Steeple Mark (not shown), circa late 1800s; German.

PLATE 454. SPINACH, Libertas, Prussia, Mark 157. Plate, 8"d, handpainted.

PLATE 455. WILD ROSE, Royal Bonn, Mark 150A; pattern is the same as Eglantine by Keller & Guerin. Cake Plate, 10"d; German.

PLATE 456. WILD ROSE, Royal Bonn, Mark 150A; Berry Set: Master Bowl, 10"d; Individual Bowl, 5'd; German.

PLATE 457. PERSIAN MOSS (correction for Plate 403 in FB1, see Williams I, p. 195), Plate, 8"d, mark 148; German.

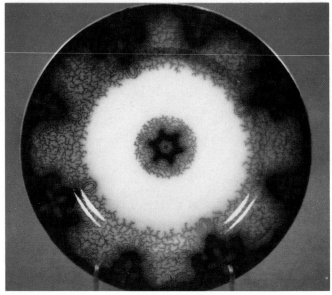

PLATE 458. Match Holder, unmarked, but porcelain body appears to be of German origin; handpainted pattern accented with red dots and gold trim; circa mid to late 1800s.

PLATE 459. Pin Dish, unmarked, porcelain body, attributed to German or other non-English origin; pink rose decorates center, deep cobalt blue border, gold trim; applied branch.

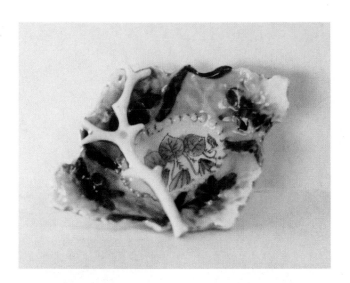

PLATE 460. Pin Dish, unmarked, similar to example in preceding photograph with variation in center decor and blue finish.

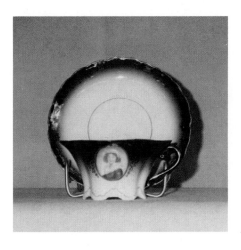

PLATE 461. Cup and Saucer decorated with cameo portrait of Madame LeBrun, unmarked, attributed to German origin.

PLATE 462. Handleless Cup, Saucer, and Plate; unmarked except for an embossed star, possibly of Dutch origin; pattern enhanced with copper lustre, circa mid 1800s.

PLATE 463. VINRANKA, Gefle, Sweden, circa late 1960s. Plate, 9½"d.

PLATE 464. VINRANKA, Gefle, Sweden. Cup and Saucer.

PLATE 465. VINRANKA, Gefle, Sweden. Cup, 2"h, and Saucer.

Reproductions

PLATE 466. Mark used by the Blakeney Pottery Company of Stoke-on-Trent, England on their "Flow Blue" wares. This confusing mark has been in use for over ten years.

PLATE 467. Muffineer made by the Blakeney Pottery Company.

PLATE 468. Covered dish made by the Blakeney Pottery Company.

PLATE 470. Wash Bowl and Pitcher set which has the "Homestead" mark.

PLATE 469. "Homestead" Mark used on modern reproductions of Flow Blue. Note "Flo Blue" printed in mark is an indication that the mark is not old.

PLATE 471. Pin Tray and set of three small flower pots (2¼" to 3"h x 3¼" to 4"w). These pieces are unmarked. They were purchased in England and appear to be part of the new wares exported from that country.

PLATE 472. Vase, unmarked. This piece represented a new item of Flow Blue in the early 1980s. It is a mold copy (except this example does not have handles) of Plate 434 in FB1.

PLATE 473. Pitcher, new import which has a gold wreath mark.

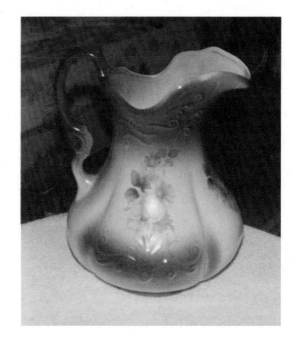

PLATE 474. Two Wash Sets representing modern English pieces which have been imported over the last ten years. One (left) has a scenic design and the other (right) has floral decoration.

Below is a list of the various items made in either the "traditional Floral pattern" or "Old English Victorian scene." This list is from an American importer's advertisement.

Bowl and pitcher sets–large
Chamber pots–large
Chamber pots–medium
Chamber pots–small
Tea pots
Coffee pots
Child size bowl & pitcher
Biscuit barrel
Shaving mug
Shoe vase

Planter
Toby pitcher
Jardinare (*sic*)
Drinking steins
Mustache cup
Toby mug
Candlesticks (pair)
Hat pin holder
Helmet cheese dish
Odd pitchers

Bibliography

Barber, William Atlee. *Marks of American Potters*, 1904.

Boger, Louise Ade. *The Dictionary of World Pottery and Porcelain*. New York: Charles Scribner's Sons, 1971.

Brink, Mrs. William. "Staffordshire," *The Encyclopedia of Collectibles*. Alexandria, Virginia: Time-Life Books, 1980.

Copeland, Robert. *Spode's Willow Pattern and Other Designs After The Chinese*. New York: Rizzoli, 1980.

Coysh, A. W. *Blue and White Transfer Ware 1780-1840*. Rutland, Vermont: Charles E. Tuttle Company, 1971.

Cushion, J. P. *Handbook of Pottery and Porcelain Marks*. London: Faber and Faber, 1980.

Fisher, S. W. *English Pottery and Porcelain Marks*. Des Moines, Iowa: Wallace-Homestead Book Co. , 1970.

Gaston, Mary Frank. *The Collector's Encyclopedia of Limoges Porcelain*. Paducah, Kentucky: Collector Books, 1983.

_____. *Blue Willow, An Illustrated Value Guide*. Paducah, Kentucky: Collector Books, 1983.

Godden, Geoffrey A. *Encyclopedia of British Pottery and Porcelain Marks*. New York: Crown Publishers, 1964.

Hughes, G. Bernard. *The Collector's Pocket Book of China*. New York: Tandem Books, 1965.

_____.*English and Scottish Earthenware*. London: Abbey Fine Arts, n.d.

Hughes, Bernard and Therle. *The Collector's Encyclopedia of English Ceramics*. London: Abbey Library, 1968.

Kovel, Ralph M. and Terry H. *Dictionary of Marks*. New York: Crown Publishers, 1953.

_____.*Kovel's New Dictionary of Marks*. New York: Crown Publishers, 1986.

Lehner, Lois. *Ohio Pottery and Glass*. Des Moines, Iowa: Wallace-Homestead Book Company, 1978.

_____.*Lehner's Encyclopedia of U.S. Marks on Pottery, Porcelain & Clay*. Paducah, Kentucky: Collector Books, 1988.

Little, W. L. *Staffordshire Blue*, London: B. T. Batsford, Ltd., 1969.

Mankowitz, Wolf and Reginald G. Haggar. *The Concise Encyclopedia of English Pottery and Porcelain*. New York: Hawthorn Books, Inc., n.d.

Mason, Veneita. *Popular Patterns of Flow Blue China with Prices*. Des Moines, Iowa: Wallace-Homestead Book Company, 1982.

Mountfield, David. *The Antique Collectors' Illustrated Dictionary*. London: Hamlyn, 1974.

Nix, Thomas. *Abbie's Flow Blue Price Guide Survey, 1991-92*. Sentinel Publishing, February 1992.

Norbury, James. *The Work of Victoriana*. London: Hamlyn, 1972.

Poche, Emanuel. *Porcelain Marks of the World*. New York: Arco Publishing Company, Inc., 1974.

Sandon, Henry. *Royal Worcester Porcelain From 1862 to the Present Day*. London: Barrie & Jenkins, 1973.

Snyder, Jeffrey B. *Flow Blue, A Collector's Guide to Pattern, History, and Values*. West Chester, Pennsylvania: Schiffer Publishing, Ltd., 1992.

Williams, Petra. *Flow Blue China An Aid To Identification*. Jeffersontown, Kentucky: Fountain House East, 1971.

_____.*Flow Blue China II*. Jeffersontown, Kentucky: Fountain House East, 1973.

_____.*Flow Blue China and Mulberry Ware*. Jeffersontown, Kentucky: Fountain House East, 1975.

Price Guide
Prices are not quoted for Reproductions, Plates 466 through 476

Plate 1 ....$175.00 – $225.00	Plate 35 ....$20.00 – $25.00
Plate 2 ....$50.00 – $60.00	Plate 36 ....$30.00 – $35.00
Plate 3 ....$50.00 – $60.00	Plate 37 ....$70.00 – $80.00
Plate 4 ....$100.00 – $125.00	Plate 38 ....$60.00 – $70.00
Plate 5 ....$30.00 – $40.00	Plate 39 ....$350.00 – $450.00
Plate 6 ....$55.00 – $65.00	Plate 40 .... $80.00 – $100.00
Plate 7 ....$40.00 – $50.00	Plate 41
Plate 8 ....$40.00 – $50.00	Tureen.............................. $300.00 – $350.00
Plate 9 ....$600.00 – $700.00	Underplate.......................$150.00 – $200.00
Plate 10...................................see Plate 9	Plate 42 ....$400.00 – $500.00
Plate 11 ....$600.00 – $700.00	Plate 43 ....$80.00 – $100.00
Plate 12 ....$1,000.00 – $1,200.00	Plate 44 ....$120.00 – $140.00
Plate 13 ....$450.00 – $550.00	Plate 45 ....$700.00 – $900.00
Plate 14 ....$350.00 – $450.00	Plate 46 ....$100.00 – $120.00
Plate 15...............................see Plate 14	Plate 47 ....set $1,200.00 – $1,400.00
Plate 16 ....$200.00 – $250.00	Plate 48 ....$450.00 – $550.00
Plate 17..........................pair $200.00 – $250.00	Plate 49 ....$350.00 – $450.00
Plate 18 ....$60.00 – $70.00	Plate 50 ....$100.00 – $120.00
Plate 19 ....set $80.00 – $90.00	Plate 51 ....$600.00 – $700.00
Plate 20 ....$140.00 – $160.00	Plate 52 ....$100.00 – $120.00
Plate 21 ....$125.00 – $150.00	Plate 53 ....each $800.00 – $1,000.00
Plate 22 ....$325.00 – $375.00	Plate 54 ....$80.00 – $100.00
Plate 23 ....$60.00 – $70.00	Plate 55 ....$175.00 – $225.00
Plate 24 ....$40.00 – $50.00	Plate 56 ....$300.00 – $400.00
Plate 25 ....$80.00 – $100.00	Plate 57 ....$600.00 – $700.00
Plate 26 ....$800.00 – $900.00	Plate 58 ....$75.00 – $85.00
Plate 27 ....$140.00 – $160.00	Plate 59 ....$100.00 – $120.00
Plate 28	Plate 60 ....$100.00 – $120.00
Tureen...................... $1,200.00 – $1,400.00	Plate 61 ....$65.00 – $75.00
Platter ....$1,000.00 – $1,200.00	Plate 62 ....$100.00 – $120.00
Ladle..............................$300.00 – $400.00	Plate 63 ....see Plate 62
Plate 29 ....set $1,400.00 – $1,600.00	Plate 64 ....$800.00 – $1,000.00
Plate 30 ....$700.00 – $800.00	Plate 65 ....$20.00 – $25.00
Plate 31 ....$800.00 – $1,000.00	Plate 66 ....$75.00 – $85.00
Plate 32 ....set $225.00 – $275.00	Plate 67
Plate 33 ....$700.00 – $800.00	Platter ....$150.00 – $175.00
Plate 34 ....$75.00 – $85.00	Covered Vegetable Bowl .....$250.00 – $300.00

Plate 68 ....$45.00 – $55.00

Plate 69 ....$1,000.00 – $1,200.00

Plate 70 ....$600.00 – $700.00

Plate 71 ....$140.00 – $160.00

Plate 72 ....$75.00 – $85.00

Plate 73 ....$250.00 – $300.00

Plate 74 ....see Plate 73

Plate 75 ....$350.00 – $450.00

Plate 76 ....$50.00 – $60.00

Plate 77 ....$350.00 – $450.00

Plate 78 ....$1,000.00 – $1,200.00

Plate 79 ....$700.00 – $800.00

Plate 80 ....$350.00 – $450.00

Plate 81 ....$275.00 – $325.00

Plate 82

    Tureen .... $225.00 – $275.00

    Underplate ....$125.00 – $175.00

    Ladle ....$120.00 – $140.00

Plate 83 ....$100.00 – $110.00

Plate 84 ....$120.00 – $130.00

Plate 85 ....(with lid) $700.00 – $800.00

Plate 86 ....$325.00 – $375.00

Plate 87 ....set $800.00 – $1,000.00

Plate 88 ....$400.00 – $500.00

Plate 89 ....see Plate 88

Plate 90 ....$500.00 – $600.00

Plate 91 ....$120.00 – $140.00

Plate 92 ....$140.00 – $160.00

Plate 93 .... set $150.00 – $175.00

Plate 94 ....$75.00 – $85.00

Plate 95 ....$75.00 – $85.00

Plate 96 ....$140.00 – $160.00

Plate 97 ....$225.00 – $275.00

Plate 98 ....$275.00 – $325.00

Plate 99 ....$450.00 – $550.00

Plate 100 ....$25.00 – $30.00

Plate 101 ....$40.00 – $50.00

Plate 102 ....$50.00 – $60.00

Plate 103 ....$80.00 – $90.00

Plate 104 ....$100.00 – $120.00

Plate 105 ....$275.00 – $325.00

Plate 106 ....$150.00 – $175.00

Plate 107

    Cov. Vegetable Bowl ......$250.00 – $300.00

    Underplate ....$175.00 – $225.00

Plate 108 ....$350.00 – $450.00

Plate 109

    Toothbrush Holder ....$250.00 – $275.00

    Pitcher ....$300.00 – $400.00

    Covered Soap Dish ....$275.00 – $300.00

    Shaving Mug ....$150.00 – $175.00

Plate 110 .... set $1,400.00 – $1,600.00

Plate 111 ....$700.00 – $800.00

Plate 112 .... (mc) $500.00 – $600.00

Plate 113

    Cov. Vegetable Bowl ....$275.00 – $300.00

Plate 114 ....$120.00 – $140.00

Plate 115 ....$150.00 – $200.00

Plate 116 ....$25.00 – $35.00

Plate 117 ....$350.00 – $450.00

Plate 118 ....$70.00 – $80.00

Plate 119 ....$800.00 – $1,000.00

Plate 120 ....$65.00 – $75.00

Plate 121 ....$125.00 – $150.00

Plate 122 ....$325.00 – $375.00

Plate 123 ....$300.00 – $350.00

Plate 124 ....$120.00 – $140.00

Plate 125 ....$125.00 – $150.00

Plate 126 ....$30.00 – $35.00

Plate 127 ....$20.00 – $25.00

Plate 128 ....$225.00 – $275.00

Plate 129 ....$400.00 – $500.00

Plate 130 ....$80.00 – $90.00

Plate 131 ....$125.00 – $150.00

Plate 132 ....$120.00 – $140.00

Plate 133 ....$25.00 – $30.00

Plate 134 ....$40.00 – $50.00

Plate 135 ....$75.00 – $85.00

Plate 136 ....$600.00 – $700.00
Plate 137 ....$60.00 – $70.00
Plate 138 ....$1,000.00 – $1,200.00
Plate 139 ....$600.00 – $700.00
Plate 140 ....$200.00 – $250.00
Plate 141 ....$80.00 – $90.00
Plate 142 ....$30.00 – $40.00
Plate 143 ....$200.00 – $250.00
Plate 144 ....$400.00 – $500.00
Plate 145 ....$65.00 – $75.00
Plate 146 ....$80.00 – $90.00
Plate 147 ....$80.00 – $90.00
Plate 148 ....$45.00 – $55.00
Plate 149 ....$350.00 – $400.00
Plate 150 ....$80.00 – $90.00
Plate 151 ....$30.00 – $40.00
Plate 152 ....$200.00 – $250.00
Plate 153 ....$40.00 – $50.00
Plate 154 ....$400.00 – $500.00
Plate 155 ....$500.00 – $600.00
Plate 156 ....$75.00 – $85.00
Plate 157 ....$200.00 – $250.00
Plate 158 ....$70.00 – $80.00
Plate 159 ....$325.00 – $375.00
Plate 160 ....$80.00 – $90.00
Plate 161 ....$40.00 – $50.00
Plate 162 ....$100.00 – $120.00
Plate 163 ....$400.00 – $500.00
Plate 164 ....$400.00 – $500.00
Plate 165 .... set $150.00 – $175.00
Plate 166 ....$800.00 – $1,000.00
Plate 167 ....$120.00 – $140.00
Plate 168 ....$80.00 – $100.00
Plate 169 ....$120.00 – $140.00
Plate 170 ....$100.00 – $120.00
Plate 171
    left .... $300.00 – $350.00
    right ....$250.00 – $300.00
Plate 172 ....$700.00 – $800.00

Plate 173 ....$80.00 – $90.00
Plate 174 ....$225.00 – $275.00
Plate 175 ....$250.00 – $300.00
Plate 176 .... set $150.00 – $175.00
Plate 177 ....$70.00 – $80.00
Plate 178 ....$200.00 – $250.00
Plate 179 ....$80.00 – $100.00
Plate 180 ....$250.00 – $300.00
Plate 181 ....$350.00 – $400.00
Plate 182 .... pair $800.00 – $1000.00
Plate 183 ....$80.00 – $100.00
Plate 184
    Cov. Vegetable Bowl ....$250.00 – $300.00
    Tray ....$200.00 – $250.00
Plate 185 ....$500.00 – $600.00
Plate 186 ....$100.00 – $125.00
Plate 187 ....$125.00 – $150.00
Plate 188 ....$300.00 – $350.00
Plate 189 ....$150.00 – $175.00
Plate 190 ....$45.00 – $55.00
Plate 191 ....$250.00 – $275.00
Plate 192 ....$45.00 – $55.00
Plate 193 ....$100.00 – $120.00
Plate 194 ....$40.00 – $50.00
Plate 195 ....$55.00 – $65.00
Plate 196 ....$60.00 – $70.00
Plate 197 ....$250.00 – $300.00
Plate 198
    Tureen .... $300.00 – $350.00
    Ladle ....$125.00 – $150.00
Plate 199 ....$200.00 – $250.00
Plate 200 ....$70.00 – $80.00
Plate 201 ....$65.00 – $75.00
Plate 202 ....$150.00 – $175.00
Plate 203 ....$130.00 – $150.00
Plate 204 ....$40.00 – $50.00
Plate 205 ....$800.00 – $1,000.00
Plate 206 ....$200.00 – $250.00
Plate 207 ....$90.00 – $100.00

Plate 208 ....$25.00 – $30.00

Plate 209 ....$20.00 – $25.00

Plate 210 ....$100.00 – $125.00

Plate 211 ....$55.00 – $65.00

Plate 212 ....$65.00 – $75.00

Plate 213 ....$75.00 – $85.00

Plate 214 ....$75.00 – $85.00

Plate 215 .... see Plate 216

Plate 216 ....set $100.00 – $125.00

Plate 217 ....$30.00 – $40.00

Plate 218 ....$40.00 – $50.00

Plate 219 ....$125.00 – $150.00

Plate 220

    Complete Service .....$3,000.00 – $3,500.00

Plate 221 ....see Plate 220

Plate 222 ....see Plate 220

Plate 223 ....see Plate 220

Plate 224 ....$80.00 – $100.00

Plate 225 ....$75.00 – $85.00

Plate 226 ....(mc) $600.00 – $700.00

Plate 227 ....$800.00 – $1,000.00

Plate 228 ....$80.00 – $100.00

Plate 229 ....$60.00 – $70.00

Plate 230 ....$250.00 – $300.00

Plate 231 ....$400.00 – $500.00

Plate 232 ....$120.00 – $140.00

Plate 233 ....$100.00 – $125.00

Plate 234 ....(mc) $400.00 – $500.00

Plate 235 ....$700.00 – $800.00

Plate 236 ....$1,400.00 – $1,600.00

Plate 237

    Shaving Mug .... $175.00 – $200.00

    Covered Soap Dish ....$275.00 – $300.00

    Toothbrush Holder ....$250.00 – $275.00

    Pitcher ....$350.00 – $450.00

Plate 238 ....$100.00 – $125.00

Plate 239 ....$100.00 – $125.00

Plate 240 ....$400.00 – $500.00

Plate 241 ....$450.00 – $550.00

Plate 242 ....$250.00 – $300.00

Plate 243 ....$55.00 – $65.00

Plate 244

    Plate .... $65.00 – $75.00

    Cup & Saucer ....$80.00 – $100.00

Plate 245 ....$120.00 – $140.00

Plate 246

    Plate ....$75.00 – $85.00

    Handleless Cup & Saucer ...$140.00 – $160.00

    Cup Plate ....$80.00 – $100.00

Plate 247 ....$250.00 – $300.00

Plate 248 ....$60.00 – $70.00

Plate 249 ....$600.00 – $700.00

Plate 250 ....$275.00 – $325.00

Plate 251 ....$450.00 – $550.00

Plate 252 .... set $400.00 – $500.00

Plate 253

    center .... $275.00 – $325.00

    right .... $225.00 – $275.00

    left ....$175.00 – $225.00

Plate 254 ....$65.00 – $75.00

Plate 255 ....$75.00 – $85.00

Plate 256 ....$70.00 – $80.00

Plate 257 ....$75.00 – $85.00

Plate 258 ....$35.00 – $45.00

Plate 259 ....$100.00 – $120.00

Plate 260 ....$65.00 – $75.00

Plate 261 ....$65.00 – $75.00

Plate 262 ....$100.00 – $120.00

Plate 263 ....$100.00 – $120.00

Plate 264 ....$250.00 – $300.00

Plate 265

    Tureen............................... $400.00 – $500.00

    Ladle..................................$150.00 – $175.00

Plate 266...see Plate 265

Plate 267 ....$130.00 – $150.00

Plate 268 .... (with lid) $800.00 – $1,000.00

Plate 269 ....$700.00 – $800.00

Plate 270 ....$275.00 – $325.00

Plate 271 ....$40.00 – $50.00

Plate 272 ....$75.00 – $100.00

Plate 273 .... set $130.00 – $150.00
Plate 274 ....$275.00 – $300.00
Plate 275 ....$350.00 – $400.00
Plate 276 ....$225.00 – $275.00
Plate 277 ....$70.00 – $80.00
Plate 278 .... set $1,800.00 – $2,000.00
Plate 279...................................see Plate 278
Plate 280...................................see Plate 278
Plate 281 ....$275.00 – $325.00
Plate 282 ....$200.00 – $250.00
Plate 283 ....$1,000.00 – $1,200.00
Plate 284 ....$300.00 – $350.00
Plate 285 ....$400.00 – $500.00
Plate 286 ....$200.00 – $225.00
Plate 287 .... (with lid) $700.00 – $800.00
Plate 288 ....$150.00 – $200.00
Plate 289 ....$125.00 – $150.00
Plate 290 ....$140.00 – $160.00
Plate 291 ....$140.00 – $160.00
Plate 292 ....$700.00 – $800.00
Plate 293 ....$700.00 – $900.00
Plate 294 ....$120.00 – $140.00
Plate 295 ....$125.00 – $150.00
Plate 296 ....$350.00 – $450.00
Plate 297 ....$100.00 – $120.00
Plate 298 ....$600.00 – $700.00
Plate 299
    Plate .... $80.00 – $100.00
    Pitchers.................. each $150.00 – $175.000
    Cup ....$45.00 – $55.00
Plate 300
    Sugar............................. $125.00 – $150.00
    Pitcher ....$150.00 – $175.00
    Tea Pot...........................$225.00 – $275.00
    Cup & Saucer ....$70.00 – $80.00
Plate 301 ....$20.00 – $25.00
Plate 302 .... set $140.00 – $160.00
Plate 303 ....$400.00 – $450.00

Plate 304
    Sugar............................... $150.00 – $175.00
    Pitcher ....$200.00 – $250.00
Plate 305
    Shaving Mug.....................$175.00 – $200.00
    large Pitcher.....................$400.00 – $500.00
    small Pitcher.....................$250.00 – $300.00
Plate 306 ....$70.00 – $80.00
Plate 307 ....$75.00 – $85.00
Plate 308 ....$20.00 – $25.00
Plate 309 ....$250.00 – $300.00
Plate 310 ....$150.00 – $175.00
Plate 311 ....$225.00 – $275.00
Plate 312
    Platter 15" x 13" ....$800.00 – $1,000.00
    Platter 41" x 33" ....$3,000.00 – $4,000.00
Plate 313
    Tureen............................. $600.00 – $800.00
    Underplate ....$400.00 – $500.00
    Ladle................................$200.00 – $250.00
Plate 314 ....$130.00 – $150.00
Plate 315 ....$700.00 – $800.00
Plate 316 ....$120.00 – $140.00
Plate 317 left, ... $275.00 – $325.00
    center ....$300.00 – $350.00
    right ....$350.00 – $400.00
Plate 318...............................$100.00 – $125.00
Plate 319 ....$350.00 – $450.00
Plate 320 ....$800.00 – $1,000.00
Plate 321 ....$20.00 – $25.00
Plate 322 ....$100.00 – $125.00
Plate 323 ....$30.00 – $40.00
Plate 324 ....$275.00 – $325.00
Plate 325 ....$225.00 – $275.00
Plate 326 ....$400.00 – $500.00
Plate 327 ....$80.00 – $90.00
Plate 328 ....$450.00 – $550.00
Plate 329 ....$125.00 – $150.00
Plate 330 ....$700.00 – $900.00

Plate 331 ....$600.00 – $700.00

Plate 332 ....$70.00 – $80.00

Plate 333 ....$55.00 – $65.00

Plate 334 ....$30.00 – $35.00

Plate 335 ....$20.00 – $25.00

Plate 336 .... set $1,400.00 – $1,600.00

Plate 337 ....$350.00 – $450.00

Plate 338

   Shaving Mug ....$150.00 – $175.00

   Toothbrush Holder ....$250.00 – $275.00

   Covered Soap Dish ....$275.00 – $300.00

   Pitcher ....$300.00 – $400.00

Plate 339 ....$700.00 – $800.00

Plate 340 ....$30.00 – $40.00

Plate 341

   left .... $175.00 – $225.00

   right ....$125.00 – $150.00

Plate 342 ....$350.00 – $450.00

Plate 343 ....$225.00 – $275.00

Plate 344 ....$300.00 – $400.00

Plate 345 ....$65.00 – $75.00

Plate 346 ....$65.00 – $75.00

Plate 347 ....$120.00 – $140.00

Plate 348

   Tea Pot .... $300.00 – $400.00

   Sugar ....$150.00 – $175.00

   Creamer ....$175.00 – $200.00

Plate 349 ....$500.00 – $600.00

Plate 350 ....$600.00 – $700.00

Plate 351

   Tureen .... $400.00 – $500.00

   Underplate ....$175.00 – $225.00

Plate 352 ....$400.00 – $500.00

Plate 353 ....$400.00 – $500.00

Plate 354 ....$120.00 – $140.00

Plate 355 ....$150.00 – $175.00

Plate 356 ....$500.00 – $600.00

Plate 357 ....$140.00 – $160.00

Plate 358 ....$125.00 – $150.00

Plate 359 ....$55.00 – $65.00

Plate 360 ....$75.00 – $85.00

Plate 361 ....$35.00 – $45.00

Plate 362 ....$300.00 – $400.00

Plate 363 ....$125.00 – $150.00

Plate 364 ....$50.00 – $60.00

Plate 365 ....$300.00 – $400.00

Plate 366 ....$500.00 – $600.00

Plate 367 ....$500.00 – $600.00

Plate 368 ....$80.00 – $90.00

Plate 369 ....$700.00 – $800.00

Plate 370 ....$30.00 – $35.00

Plate 371 ....$200.00 – $250.00

Plate 372 ....$40.00 – $50.00

Plate 373 ....$80.00 – $100.00

Plate 374 ....$80.00 – $100.00

Plate 375 ....$120.00 – $140.00

Plate 376 ....$80.00 – $100.00

Plate 377 ....$80.00 – $100.00

Plate 378 ....$150.00 – $175.00

Plate 379

   Sugar .... $150.00 – $157.00

   Creamer ....$175.00 – $200.00

Plate 380 ....$140.00 – $160.00

Plate 381 ....$140.00 – $160.00

Plate 382 ....$30.00 – $35.00

Plate 383 ....$200.00 – $250.00

Plate 384 ....$250.00 – $300.00

Plate 385 .... $75.00 – $85.00

Plate 386 ....set $1,200.00 – $1,400.00

Plate 387 ....see Plate 386

Plate 388 ....$500.00 – $600.00

Plate 389 ....$150.00 – $175.00

Plate 390 ....$200.00 – $250.00

Plate 391 ....$40.00 – $50.00

Plate 392 ....$175.00 – $225.00

Plate 393 ....$150.00 – $200.00

Plate 394 ....$175.00 – $225.00

Plate 395 ....$250.00 – $350.00

Plate 396 ....$600.00 – $700.00

Plate 397 ....$350.00 – $400.00

Plate 398 ....$175.00 – $225.00

Plate 399 ....$175.00 – $225.00

Plate 400.................................see Plate 399

Plate 401 ....$325.00 – $375.00

Plate 402 .... set $1,400.00 – $1,600.00

Plate 403 .... set $1,200.00 – $1,400.00

Plate 404 ....$80.00 – $100.00

Plate 405 ....$70.00 – $90.00

Plate 406 ....$80.00 – $100.00

Plate 407 ....$140.00 – $160.00

Plate 408 ....$80.00 – $100.00

Plate 409 ....$125.00 – $150.00

Plate 410 ....$100.00 – $120.00

Plate 411 ....$100.00 – $125.00

Plate 412 ....$200.00 – $250.00

Plate 413 .... each $250.00 – $300.00

Plate 414 ....$100.00 – $120.00

Plate 415 ....$140.00 – $160.00

Plate 416 ....$80.00 – $100.00

Plate 417 .... each $100.00 – $120.00

Plate 418 ....$300.00 – $400.00

Plate 419................................see Plate 418

Plate 420 ....$550.00 – $650.00

Plate 421 ....$50.00 – $60.00

Plate 422 ....$120.00 – $140.00

Plate 423 ....$25.00 – $35.00

Plate 424 ....$55.00 – $65.00

Plate 425 ....$50.00 – $60.00

Plate 426 ....$55.00 – $65.00

Plate 427 ....$55.00 – $65.00

Plate 428 ....$50.00 – $60.00

Plate 429 ....$175.00 – $225.00

Plate 430 ....$80.00 – $100.00

Plate 431 ....$55.00 – $65.00

Plate 432 ....$400.00 – $500.00

Plate 433 ....$65.00 – $75.00

Plate 434 ....$250.00 – $300.00

Plate 435 ....$300.00 – $400.00

Plate 436 .... each $80.00 – $100.00

Plate 437 ....$100.00 – $125.00

Plate 438 ....$40.00 – $50.00

Plate 439 ....$25.00 – $30.00

Plate 440 ....$150.00 – $175.00

Plate 441 ....$125.00 – $150.00

Plate 442 ....$500.00 – $600.00

Plate 443 ....$275.00 – $325.00

Plate 444 ....$200.00 – $250.00

Plate 445 ....$40.00 – $50.00

Plate 446 ....$400.00 – $500.00

Plate 447 ....see Plate 446

Plate 448 ....$80.00 – $100.00

Plate 449 ....$350.00 – $450.00

Plate 450 ....$120.00 – $140.00

Plate 451 ....$45.00 – $55.00

Plate 452 ....$300.00 – $400.00

Plate 453 ....$175.00 – $225.00

Plate 454 ....$50.00 – $60.00

Plate 455 ....$125.00 – $150.00

Plate 456

  Master Bowl .... $150.00 – $200.00

  Individual Bowls ....$30.00 – $40.00

Plate 457 ....$50.00 – $60.00

Plate 458 .... $150.00 – $200.00

Plate 459 ....$125.00 – $150.00

Plate 460 ....$125.00 – $150.00

Plate 461 ....$150.00 – $175.00

Plate 462

  Plate .... $65.00 – $75.00

  Handleless Cup & Saucer.$120.00 – $140.00

Plate 463 ....$45.00 – $55.00

Plate 464 ....$65.00 – $75.00

Plate 465 ....$65.00 – $75.00

COLLECTOR BOOKS

I n f o r m i n g   T o d a y ' s   C o l l e c t o r

For over two decades we have been keeping collectors informed on trends and values in all fields of antiques and collectibles.

The following is a partial listing of our books on pottery, porcelain, and figurines:

e and White Stoneware-McNerney-5½x8½-152 Pgs.-(PB) ....#1312/$ 9.95
e Ridge Dinnerware, Revised 3rd Ed.-Newbound-8½x11-160 Pgs.-(PB) ....#1958/$14.95
e Willow, Revised 2nd Ed.-Gaston-8½x11-169 Pgs.-(HB) ....#1959/$14.95
ectible Vernon Kilns-Nelson-8½x11-256 Pgs.-(HB) ....#3816/$24.95
ecting Yellow Ware-McAllister-8½x11-128 Pgs.-(HB) ....#3311/$16.95
ector's Ency. of American Dinnerware-Cunningham-8½x11-322 Pgs.-(HB) ....#1373/$24.95
ector's Ency. of Blue Ridge Dinnerware-Newbound-8½x11-176 Pgs.-(HB) ....#3815/$19.95
ector's Ency. of California Pottery-Chipman-8½x11-160 Pgs.-(HB) ....#2272/$24.95
ector's Ency. of Colorado Pottery-Carlton-8½x11-168 Pgs.-(HB) ....#3811/$24.95
ector's Ency. of Cookie Jars-Roerig-8½x11-312 Pgs.-(HB) ....#2133/$24.95
ector's Ency. of Cookie Jars, Vol II-Roerig-8½x11-400 Pgs-(HB) ....#3723/$24.95
ector's Ency. of Cowan Pottery-Saloff-8½x11-176 Pgs.-(HB) ....#3429/$24.95
ector's Ency. of Early Noritake-Alden-8½x11-216 Pgs.-(HB) ....#3961/$24.95
ector's Ency. of Fiesta-Huxford-8½x11-190 Pgs.-(HB) ....#2209/$19.95
ector's Ency. of Flow Blue China-Gaston-8½x11-160 Pgs.-(HB) ....#1439/$19.95
ector's Ency. of Flow Blue China, 2nd Edition-Gaston-8½x11-184 Pgs.-(HB) ....#3812/$24.95
ector's Ency. of Hall China, 2nd Edition-Whitmyer-8½x11-272 Pgs.-(HB) ....#3813/$24.95
ector's Ency. of Homer Laughlin China-Jasper-8½x11-208 Pgs.-(HB) ....#3431/$24.95
ector's Ency. of Hull Pottery-Roberts-8½x11-207 Pgs.-(HB) ....#1276/$19.95
ector's Ency. of Lefton China-DeLozier-8½x11-144 Pgs.-(HB) ....#3962/$19.95
ector's Ency. of Limoges Porcelain, 2nd Ed.-Gaston-8½x11-224 Pgs.-(HB) ....#2210/$24.95
ector's Ency. of Majolica-Katz-Marks-8½x11-192 Pgs.-(HB) ....#2334/$19.95
ector's Ency. of Metlox Potteries-8½x11-344 Pgs.-(HB) ....#3963/$24.95
ector's Ency. of McCoy Pottery-Huxford-8½x11-247 Pgs.-(HB) ....#1358/$19.95
ector's Ency. of Niolak-Gifford-8½x11-256 Pgs.-(HB) ....#3313/$19.95
ector's Ency. of Nippon Porcelain I-Van Patten-8½x11-222 Pgs.-(HB) ....#3837/$24.95
ector's Ency. of Nippon Porcelain, 2nd Series-Van Patten-8½x11-256 Pgs.-(HB) ....#2089/$24.95
ector's Ency. of Nippon Porcelain, 3rd Series-Van Patten-8½x11-320 Pgs.-(HB) ....#1665/$24.95
ector's Ency. of Noritake-Van Patten-8½x11-200 Pgs.-(HB) ....#1447/$19.95
ector's Ency. of Noritake, 2nd Series-Van Patten-8½x11-264 Pgs.-(HB) ....#3432/$24.95
ector's Ency. of Occupied Japan, Vol. I-Florence-8½x11-108 Pgs.-(PB) ....#1037/$14.95
ector's Ency. of Occupied Japan, Vol. II-Florence-8½x11-112 Pgs.-(PB) ....#1038/$14.95
ector's Ency. of Occupied Japan, Vol. III-Florence-8½x11-144 Pgs.-(PB) ....#2088/$14.95
ector's Ency. of Occupied Japan, Vol. IV-Florence-8½x11-128 Pgs.-(PB) ....#2019/$14.95
ector's Ency. of Occupied Japan, Vol. V-Florence-8½x11-128 Pgs.-(PB) ....#2335/$14.95
ector's Ency. of Pickard China-Reed-8½x11-336 Pgs.-(HB) ....#3964/$24.95
ector's Ency. of R.S. Prussia, 1st Series-Gaston-8½x11-216 Pgs.-(HB) ....#1311/$24.95
ector's Ency. of R.S. Prussia, 2nd Series-Gaston-8½x11-230 Pgs.-(HB) ....#1715/$24.95
ector's Ency. of R.S. Prussia, 3rd Series-Gaston-8½x11-224 Pgs.-(HB) ....#3726/$24.95

Collector's Ency. of R.S. Prussia, 4th Series-Gaston-8½x11-288 Pgs.-(HB) ....#3877/$24.95
Collector's Ency. of Roseville Pottery-Huxford-8½x11-192 Pgs.-(HB) ....#1034/$19.95
Collector's Ency. of Roseville Pottery, Vol. 2-Huxford-8½x11-207 Pgs.-(HB) ....#1035/$19.95
Collector's Ency. of Russel Wright Designs-Kerr-8½x11-192 Pgs.-(HB) ....#2083/$19.95
Collector's Ency. of Sascha Brastoff-Conti, Bethany, Seay-8½x11-320 Pgs.-(HB) ....#3965/$24.95
Collector's Ency. of Van Briggle Art Pottery-Sasicki & Fania-8½x11-144 Pgs.-(HB) ....#3314/$24.95
Collector's Ency. of Wall Pockets-Newbound-8½x11-192 Pgs.-(HB) ....#4563/$19.95
Collector's Ency. of Weller Pottery-Huxford-8½x11-375 Pgs.-(HB) ....#2111/$29.95
Collector's Guide to Country Stoneware & Pottery-Raycraft-5½x8½-160 Pgs.-(PB) ....#3452/$11.95
Collector's Guide to Country Stoneware & Pottery, 2nd Series-Raycraft-8½x11-375 Pgs-(PB)-.#2077/$14.95
Collector's Guide to Harker Pottery-Colbert-8½x11-128 Pgs.-(PB) ....#3433/$17.95
Collector's Guide to Hull Pottery, The Dinnerware Lines-Gick-Burke-8½x11-168 Pgs.-(PB)..#3434/$16.95
Collector's Guide to Lu-Ray Pastels-Meehan-8½x11-160 Pgs.-(PB) ....#3876/$18.95
Collector's Guide to Made in Japan Ceramics-White-8½x11-214 Pgs.-(PB) ....#3814/$18.95
Collector's Guide to Rockingham-Brewer-5½x8½-128 Pgs.-(PB) ....#4565/$14.95
Collector's Guide to Shawnee Pottery-Vanderbilt-8½x11-144 Pgs.-(HB) ....#2339/$19.95
Cookie Jars-Westfall-5½x8½-160 Pgs.-(PB) ....#1425/$ 9.95
Cookie Jars, Book II-Westfall-8½x11-256 Pgs.-(PB) ....#3440/$19.95
Debolt's Dictionary of American Pottery Marks-DeBolt-8½x11-288 Pgs.-(PB) ....#3435/$17.95
Early Roseville-Huxford-5½x8½-72 Pgs.-(PB) ....#2076/$ 7.95
Head Vases-Cole-8½x11-142 Pgs.-(PB) ....#1917/$14.95
Lehner's Ency. of U.S. Marks on Pottery, Porcelain & Clay-Lehner-8½x11-644 Pgs.-(HB) ....#2379/$24.95
Purinton Pottery-Morris-8½x11-272 Pgs.-(HB) ....#3825/$24.95
Red Wing Stoneware-DePasquale-5½x8½-160 Pgs.-(PB) ....#1440/$ 9.95
Red Wing Collectibles-DePasquale-5½x8½-160 Pgs.-(PB) ....#1670/$ 9.95
Royal Copley-Wolfe-5½x8½-136 Pgs.-(PB) ....#2350/$14.95
More Royal Copley-Wolfe-5½x8½-128 Pgs.-(PB) ....#2351/$14.95
Shawnee Pottery-Mangus-8½x11-256 Pgs.-(HB) ....#3738/$24.95
Wall Pockets of the Past-Perkins-8½x11-160 Pgs.-(PB) ....#4572/$17.95
Watt Pottery Id. & Value Guide-Morris-8½x11-160 Pgs.-(HB) ....#3327/$19.95

This is only a partial listing of the books on pottery and porcelain that are available from Collector Books. All books are well illustrated and contain current values. Most of the following books are available from your local bookseller, antique dealer, or public library. If you are unable to locate certain titles in your area, you may order by mail from COLLECTOR BOOKS, P.O. Box 3009, Paducah, KY 42002-3009. Customers with Visa or MasterCard may phone in orders from 7:00–4:00 CST, Monday–Friday, Toll Free 1-800-626-5420. Add $2.00 for postage for the first book ordered and $0.30 for each additional book. Include item number, title, and price when ordering. Allow 14 to 21 days for delivery.

E CARRY MORE THAN 300 BOOKS ON ANTIQUES & COLLECTIBLES • SEND FOR A FREE, COMPLETE LISTING OF ALL OUR TITLES